Credit Score Hacks

A Step-by-Step Guide to Rebuilding Your Credit, Raising Your Score, and Increasing Your Business (2022 Guide For Beginners)

Theo Webster

Content List

Introduction

Do you know what your credit score is? You really should. A credit score can determine your eligibility for life's nuts and bolts. Your credit score influences your ability to buy a home, get a good interest rate on loan, or even find a new job. It refers to the risk of non-payment that you present to a lender.

This book is written with the goal of providing information that is as accurate and reliable as possible. This book will teach you everything there is to know about credit and what to avoid. You will learn how to identify negative items in your credit reports and important strategies for cleaning up your credit reports. Remember that if you have bad credit, you are not completely helpless and hopeless. You have the ability to repair your credit on your own.

After you've repaired your credit, you can use the advice in this book to keep your credit record clean at all times, learn how to rebuild your credit and work toward financial independence. These are not difficult steps to take. All you have to do is be willing to take them.

We all want to have a good credit rating because we understand that it makes credit more accessible and affordable; therefore, we will go to any length to avoid doing anything that could jeopardize that rating.

What happens if your efforts to improve your credit rating do not yield the desired results? Credit restoration may be the best option for you. In any case, why should you pay more if you don't have to? This book will walk you through the process of repairing your credit so that all negative items are permanently removed from your credit report.

Credit is extremely important nowadays because most people use it almost every day, even without realizing it as if it were a necessary part of their daily survival. Credit cards, house payments, and car payments are just a few examples. Regrettably, many people do not think about their credit rating until they have problems dealing with it.

When you have a bad credit rating, it can have an impact on more than just your ability to obtain a loan. It may also cause difficulties in obtaining any type of credit. For example, you may encounter difficulties when renting a property, paying deposits on phone lines and other utilities, or obtaining store financing. As a result, it is critical to monitor your credit score.

If, on the other hand, you have a bad credit rating, there are several things you can do to repair your credit. The first and most important step is to obtain your credit report. You should be aware that all information about your credit is reported to credit bureaus by your bank and other financial institutions with which you are involved. In turn, the credit bureaus are the ones who hold the key to starting the credit repair process.

Unless they are in the process of credit repair, most people pay little attention to their credit reports. Regardless of your credit rating, you must obtain a copy of your credit report.

If you are attempting to repair your credit, you must first examine your credit report. In some cases, credit reports contain inaccuracies or discrepancies. For example, your credit information could have been mixed up with that of another person with the same name.

There are also instances where your credit file contains incorrect information.

Many people are taken aback when they receive reports of unintentionally missed payments.

If you discover any inaccuracies or discrepancies in your credit report, you can perform credit repair by request, usually in writing, that the relevant credit bureau investigates the disputed items. You may include supporting documentation, if available, in your request or simply state your dispute and request an investigation.

If you're struggling with bad credit due to poor decisions or something else, we'll give you some tools to help you restore your good name and get back on track. Most people struggle from time to time with a negative mark on their credit but don't be fooled into thinking there is no way back. Hopefully, by the end of this book, you'll be back on track to a viable financial future, with a more positive financial image to present to the world.

This book contains the solution you've been looking for—a chance to reclaim your life and provide you with everything you need to get back on track.

To repair a bad credit report, all you need to do is hire a professional credit repair company to do it for you or do it yourself. The do-it-yourself strategy is ideal for people who want to delve deep into the procedures and understand how the system works. In any case, the more technical aspects will almost certainly necessitate the use of a guide or manual.

Good credit can help you in life, and you can improve your score.

If you want to easily and quickly secure a loan, you must have the best credit score possible. You will also appreciate the benefits that come with it as your credit score improves. Having lower scheduled installments is one of the most significant benefits of having a good credit score.

You can improve your credit score by paying your bills on time and utilizing close to 30% of the credit you have available at any given time. You should also avoid taking out a loan unless absolutely necessary. Similarly, don't be enticed to use multiple credit extensions at the same time. Furthermore, review your credit reports at least once a year to look for any errors.

CHAPTER 1

CREDIT SCORE?

What is the story about?

WHAT EXACTLY IS A CREDIT SCORE?

The credit score is the number obtained after analyzing a person's financial records, particularly his credit history, in order to determine his creditworthiness level. It is a number that represents how well that individual manages all of the money he borrows. It is the primary determinant used by many lending institutions, alongside or in addition to the five C's of credit (character, capacity, capital, collateral, conditions). While the latter determines a person's creditworthiness, the former interpret it objectively.

Most businesses use a variety of credit assessment measures to determine the creditworthiness of potential borrowers, but the credit score is the most objective of all. Many financial and corporate decisions are aided by credit scores. Credit card companies, banks, and other financial institutions use credit scores to determine the potential risks they will face when lending money to a person.

They also use this score to assess the potential losses they may incur as a result of unpaid loans and bad debts. They also use this score to determine who is qualified to be their borrowers, the amount of money they will lend to them, the various terms and conditions they can impose on each of them, and the interest rate they can charge them.

When a person runs out of cash, for example, he has the option of obtaining credit. He can still buy using the lending company's credit card.

However, issuing a credit card necessitates a number of steps, one of which is determining his financial capability. The credit score will assist lending institutions in determining whether he is creditworthy.

Creditworthiness is a measure of a person's likelihood of meeting his financial obligations. Other countries, on the other hand, regard creditworthiness as a measure of a person's likelihood of failing to meet his financial obligations.

Creditworthiness is important in financial matters because lending companies must generate revenue in order to continue lending money. Assume they do not investigate the creditworthiness of each of their borrowers. In that case, they may face bankruptcy, either because their borrowers are cash-strapped or because they have already fled the country.

Creditworthiness serves to protect not only the lending company's but also the public's interests.

HOW DO CREDIT SCORE SYSTEMS WORK?

Understanding what your credit score is made of and how it works is the key to improving it. If you can break it down into its constituent parts, you can deal with each one separately. It makes it easier to understand what is coming from where and how to change things for the better, the best, and quickest.

HOW ARE CREDIT SCORES GENERATED?

There are numerous scoring systems available today. Each has its own proprietary algorithm and takes a different approach to things.

Each company or entity selects its own system. In some cases, they may calculate your credit score using various methods before making a decision.

FICO scores are by far the most widely used, with more than 90% of credit institutions relying on them. FICO (formerly Fair Isaac Corporation) does not reveal the proprietary algorithm used to calculate the final score. However, it is known that the formula is based on five major components, each of which is weighted according to importance.

However, as previously stated, FICO's is not the only current score calculation system available. There are a few more. Your score may differ by 100 points between systems due to differences in the calculation mechanisms used.

FICO's Scoring Model

FICO has the most dependable scoring model, thanks in large part to its long track record. Fair Isaac Company first computed these scores in 1989. They have since revised the algorithms several times over the last three decades to account for changing factors in order to produce consistently reliable credit scores.

Creditworthiness ranges between 600 and 740, indicating average to above-average creditworthiness. FICO introduced its FICO 9 scoring model in 2014.

The primary change in this model was to downplay the significance of unpaid medical bills. The reasoning behind this is that unpaid medical debts are not true indicators of financial health.

You could be waiting for insurance to pay a medical bill, or you could be completely unaware that a medical bill has been turned over to a collection agency. This critical change allowed some people's credit scores to rise by up to 25 points.

Other changes made in 2017 prohibited collectors from reporting late medical debts that were not yet 180 days past due. In 2017, the three credit reporting bureaus also removed all data on civil judgments and tax lien records from their databases. According to FICO, this improved the credit scores of approximately 6% of consumers. Prior to the release of FICO 9, the standard credit score version was FICO 8 (created by the company in 2009). FICO 8 is still the most commonly used credit score in the lending industry. FICO 8 distinguished itself by penalizing you for charging near your total credit limit each month and granting forgiveness if you had only one late payment of more than 30 days.

It is worth noting that whenever FICO releases an updated version of its scoring models, lenders can choose to keep the current version or upgrade.

Because upgrading to the new model is so expensive, FICO 8 has remained the overwhelming favorite.

Even FICO 5 models are still used by some lenders. When you go through the application process, you can ask your lender which model they are using.

FICO scores typically do not change significantly in the short term. The only exception is if you begin missing payments or accumulating charge-offs and defaults. Similarly, not everyone has a FICO score. If you do not have credit, you will be classified as having "credit invisible," according to experts.

To obtain a FICO score, you must have six months of payments reported to credit bureaus.

Many people are unaware that it is a federal law that requires you to review your credit reports at least once a year. It may appear strange, but there was a time when you would not have been permitted to see what information had been gathered about you. Because you would not have been their primary consumer, the credit bureaus felt they were not required to notify you of any information gathered about you. However, a federal law enacted about 25 years ago changed everything. You can now check each of these agencies' reports at least once a year.

If you haven't checked your report in a long time, it's a good idea to do so now. If you have checked it, it is recommended that you pull from a single agency once every four months to see what has changed on your report and make corrections as soon as they occur.

Obtaining a copy is simple. To begin, go to

AnnualCreditReport.com and follow the on-screen instructions to request your report.

COMMONLY APPLIED SCORING METHODS

We've already mentioned the FICO score, which is the most widely used method for calculating credit scores. FICO employs a number of different scoring models, each of which is designed for a specific purpose. For example, their NextGen scoring model is used to assess consumer credit risk, whereas the FICO SBSS is used to evaluate small businesses applying for credit.

FICO calculates credit scores using the three national credit bureaus.

Experian, Equifax, and TransUnion are three of them. Each of these credit bureaus may have unique information on any given consumer. These three bureaus collaborated to create their credit scoring system in order to compete with FICO. The Vantage Score differs from the FICO Score in several ways. A credit report generated with the Vantage Score may contain significantly different values than one generated with FICO. Although it is not as widely used as FICO, Vantage Score is widely accepted by the financial community.

Before making a decision, some financial institutions will obtain credit reports from both systems for a consumer. Other scoring systems are also available. CE Analytics publishes the CE Score.

Currently, over 6,000 lending institutions in the United States have access to this score.

In addition, financial institutions may choose to use non-traditional credit scores to gain a better understanding of their customers. The majority of these scores are based on information that the national credit bureaus do not have. Such credit scores may be more reliant on utility, rental, and telecommunications payment data.

Mortgages, property deeds, and tax records are examples of public record information that could be used.

SCORE VALUES FOR CREDIT

Your credit score will be assigned a numerical value each time it is calculated. The range of these values is determined by the scoring system employed.

FICO and Vantage Score 4.0 (the most recent Vantage Score model) compute a score between 300 and 850.

Other scoring systems have wildly disparate scoring ranges. However, one thing remains consistent across all orders: the higher your score, the better. While no calculation model is perfect, lenders still consider consumers with a higher rating to be less risky. It increases the likelihood that they will offer you their services and gets you a better deal.

Because FICO is by far the most popular credit score, we'll take a closer look at how their credit ranges are broken down. The FICO Score 9 model is the most recent, but many institutions continue to use the FICO 8 model, which we will discuss below.

FICO SCORE 8 RANGES AND LENDERS' PERCEPTION OF THEM SCORE RANGE CLASSIFICATION

300-559 Poor 560-669 Fair 670-739 Good 740-799 Excellent

800-850 Exceptional

HOW ARE CREDIT SCORES CALCULATED?

The factors considered when calculating your credit score determine what your credit score reads. These will differ significantly between scoring systems and even between scoring models within the same network.

As previously stated, FICO and Vantage Score, while employing different scoring algorithms, both rely on information from the three national credit bureaus. Equifax, Experian, and Transunion are the three credit reporting agencies. Other, less traditional scoring systems may use only a portion of the information available from these three credit bureaus if any at all. They may choose to rely on data that these bureaus do not have, such as rental and utility payment histories. Mortgages, liens, personal property titles, and deeds are also frequently used public record information. Each system will calculate your credit score using a specific set of data, assigning weight or importance to each component.

It usually manifests as each component contributing a certain percentage to the final score. Some factors, such as your payment history, will be heavily weighted. Other factors, such as new credit, will have a much smaller impact. This, too, varies depending on the scoring system used.

REPORT ON CREDIT

The credit report is the primary document used by lending institutions in calculating a person's credit score. It contains various personal and financial information about the individual, such as where they live, how they pay their bills, their current financial situation (whether they are bankrupt or insolvent), and whether they have been sued for money collection due to unpaid loans. A credit report is free to obtain, so before applying for credit, a person should obtain a copy of it. The Fair Credit Reporting Act (FCRA), the law that governs the reporting of a person's credit information, requires every credit reporting company or agency to provide a free copy of a person's credit report once a year upon request.

WHERE CAN I FIND A GOOD CREDIT SCORE?

It is much more difficult to qualify for a loan in today's economy. To qualify for most types of credit today, you must have an excellent credit score. So, what exactly is a good credit score rating?

850 is perfect credit and the highest credit score rating conceivable; however, I've never met anyone with an 850.

A good credit score begins in the 670s. Credit scores less than 670 are not considered good.

Credit scores typically range from 300 to 850. A lower value indicates that the individual is less creditworthy, whereas a higher value indicates that the individual is more creditworthy. However, lending companies use their respective financial data on their clients to broaden this interpretation. Instead of referring to a high or low credit score, they have created specific brackets that describe how creditworthy a person is.

The following explains what each credit score range means:

a. A credit score of 751 to 800 allows a borrower to apply for credit with the lowest interest rate and the most competitive amount because lending companies know he will not default on his financial obligations. This is widely regarded as the best possible score. Anyone who receives a score in this range can almost certainly expect their application to be approved.

b. A credit score ranging from 711 to 750 entitles a borrower to apply for credit at competitive interest rates. While the person's credit is relatively good, they will be charged a slightly higher interest rate than someone with a credit score of 751 or higher. Someone with a credit score in this range has a relatively good credit standing.

c. A credit score of 651 to 710 enables a borrower to apply for credit with low-interest rates. This is the standard score that applicants must achieve in order for their application to be approved.

d. Someone with a credit score of 581-650 may be able to apply for credit but only at high-interest rates. This is because the possibility of risks and losses increases at this level.

e. A credit score of 300-580 disqualifies a person from applying for credit.

Their application may be approved, but they will only be able to take advantage of it if they are willing to pay the highest interest rate. This is because the possibility of loss is extremely high in this range.

However, it should be noted that there is no universal method for determining a person's credit score. Its calculation is determined by the company evaluating him. His credit score may differ when assessed by different companies, but the range of scores may be interpreted to mean the same thing due to the factors taken into account when assessing him.

For example, his credit score maybe 375 in one company and 340 in another, but both indicate that he is less creditworthy and must repair his credit score quickly.

GETTING A GOOD CREDIT SCORE:

Your credit is scored based on five criteria that are fairly simple to understand.

Payment History accounts for 35% of your credit score.

Do you make on-time payments on your bills? You will have a good credit score in two years if you don't do anything else but make on-time payments. One of the most effective ways to support your credit is to avoid late payments. Otherwise, the consequences of your previous actions will continue to harm your credit score.

One continuous multi-day late payment will lower your credit score by at least 20 points! A few late payments and your credit score will plummet precipitously. Being late by several days can significantly lower your credit score, and they are a major issue when calculating your credit score. Understand that the later the wrongdoing, the greater the negative impact on your score. While there is usually a grace period, anything more than 30 days will seriously harm your credit score. Make a point of analyzing your debt and reviewing your bank statements. Make prompt payments and deal with accounts before they become overdue or go to collections. Try not to overextend yourself to the point where it jeopardizes your ability to make timely payments. If you have old late payments on your credit report that can't be removed or fixed, remember that time heals old wounds, and your score will rise if no new misconduct is reported.

Always remember to pay your credit cards before the "Grace Period" expires. Late payments are penalized by creditors. This is a tremendous benefit for the banks. A bank may charge you $30-$35 for being two hours late with your payments! (Always read the fine print on anything) Several banks have also introduced other feeds related to multi-day late payments that are triggered even before the 30 day period. Don't push your due date too close. Make your payments as soon as possible, or set up automatic payments, so you don't forget.

Amount The amount owed accounts for 30% of your credit score.

The credit scoring model determines your credit balance, which is usually calculated against your high credit limit. This is calculated in terms of rates. It is critical to keep your balances as low as possible. If you have a $5,000 credit limit on a card, keeping your balance under $500 puts you in the 10% range of available credit. There are debt proportion thresholds that will cause your credit score to rise. These percentages are 70%, 50%, 30%, and 10%, respectively. If you can't pay off your credit cards in full, pay them off BELOW the following conceivable limit.

Calculate your credit limits in accordance with these guidelines. Increase 5000 x. ten if you have a card with a $5,000 limit (or.30,.50,.70), You must pay your balance for at least these amounts. Under $500 (or $1500, $2500, or $3500) for this situation.

Remember that the main activity is to check your credit report for credit limits. If your credit limit isn't being reported, the scoring model will use your balance as your credit limit. This means you're utilizing all of your available resources. Make a call to your creditor and make sure they fix it. Conveyance of debt is a simple way to ensure you maintain a good credit score.

To limit proportion, try to have a good debt spread with a lower balance.

For example, having $2,000 in debt on five cards is preferable to having $10,000 on one card with all others paid off. If you're getting close to your credit limit, apply for more credit or request a credit increase from your current accounts.

This criterion is based on total availability rather than an estimate of availability. It makes no difference whether you require $500 or $50,000. What matters is how you handle it. Debt consolidation on additional credit cards or credit lines can help you raise your credit score quickly.

The length of your credit history accounts for 15% of your credit score.

The length of your credit history refers to the length of time you've had your credit accounts. If you've had a credit history for 15 years, it's more stable than if you've only had it for two months. A key point to remember here is to never close your credit cards. Keep your old accounts open if they are in good standing, even if you don't use them and there is no balance.

However, keep in mind that you must use your credit lines on a regular basis in order to keep them active. Accounts that have been inactive for more than six months become idle and are ignored by credit bureaus unless there is a reprobate action associated with that record—keeping your credit lines also open aids in improving your credit availability, as explained in the preceding section. If you want to include credit, ask your credit card company to raise your credit limit. Aside from getting another card, the best way to increase your credit lines is to broaden your line on an old record with a good and long history.

Make certain that they accurately report the credit amount increment to the bureaus. Long credit histories are a common feature of exceptionally good credit scores.

Credit reports with old accounts with a fifteen to twenty-year history are likely to have much higher scores. Finally, it is critical to add older stable credit lines to your report and keep them in good standing even if you are not using them.

The amount of new credit you have accounted for 10% of your credit score.

Fresh out of the box or newly opened accounts are examples of new credit. If you have only recently opened your account, you will need to gradually increase its authority. If you've recently applied for ten credit cards, banks will generally accept the possibility that you've lost your job and need a backup plan.

Begin with a small credit extension and work your way up from there. When you open a new credit line, make sure you can make the payments on time, are not late, and keep your balances as low as possible or paid off.

The type of credit used accounts for 10% of your credit score.

The credit scoring model prefers to see a variety of credit types in your file. The best credit arrangement is to have a home loan, a car payment, and a couple of credit cards. This credit is distributed across various types of lenders and types of credit that have been made available to you. There are two types of credit to avoid. Payday loans are a bad way to build credit, and having these high-risk loans will most likely harm your credit score. Other terrible types of credit are those that allow you to make no payments for a year. These are risky because the terms of the agreement usually state that if you do not pay off the loan within a year, you will owe the entire year's worth of payments at a rate of 20% interest on day 366. This is already a disaster in the making.

Individuals who take advantage of these offers on multiple occasions are likely to have credit problems. That type of credit should not be on your credit report.

WHY SHOULD YOU USE A DIFFERENT CREDIT SCORE INSTEAD OF JUST ONE?

This is a critical question with a straightforward answer. There are numerous credit scores available, just as there are numerous automobiles available, such as pickup trucks and four-door sedans.

Consider two vehicles that are roughly the same size and shape. They are hybrids that can be charged electrically or run on gasoline.

They both have four wheels, gears, steering wheels, and comfortable seats.

Nonetheless, some people will opt for one company's model while others will opt for the other.

When it comes to automobiles, everyone has different preferences. When it comes to credit scores, the situation is similar. Certain credit scores are preferred by some lenders over others. The information in your credit report is used by all credit bureaus. However, their treatment of the information varies slightly depending on the needs of specific lenders, which is why there are different ranges and credit scores.

As a result, it is critical not to become overly concerned with your credit score. The number has significance for your lender and the specific transaction you'll be conducting with them. The online credit scores are only a starting point for you to determine how creditworthy your lender believes you are. However, taking this score to the lender may not be enough to get your loan approved.

They are unlikely to base their decision and subsequent loan on the online score you provide because they may be using a different one than the one you provided. Even if you bring the score from the same credit score developer, this could happen.

A better idea would be to look at the model's range and see where you fall in that range. It is in your best interest to read the risk factors statements that come with your score carefully.

If the lender provides you with the scores, it is a good idea to obtain the risk factor statements that go along with those scores. If you have accessed the scores, you will also receive a list of what has had the greatest impact on your scores and how they turned out.

To be a less risky borrower, you should first address the issues mentioned in the risk factor statements. These statements will be very similar regardless of which credit rating companies you used to obtain them. You'll be able to improve your credit over time if you work on those issues.

No one ever has a perfect credit score because, by definition, when you have credit, you are carrying some risk. These risks will be reflected in your credit scores.

WHAT YOU SHOULD KNOW IF YOU DO NOT HAVE A CREDIT SCORE

Individuals have misbeliefs and misconceptions about credit card issues due to a lack of information. To be well-informed about credit scores and what to do if you don't have one, you need to know a few things.

It restricts your credit score options.

You must have credit in order to obtain credit. It is more difficult to find lenders who will lend to you if you do not have a credit score. Though it is not impossible to obtain credit without a credit score, lenders require proof that you can make online payments, manage funds properly, and so on before they will consider lending to you.

Starting small with a student loan can help you make regular, on-time payments while also improving your credit score.

Bad credit if you don't have a credit score.

Not having a credit score may imply that you haven't needed one, which isn't necessarily a bad thing. It also does not necessarily imply that you have a bad credit habit, as you may believe.

It takes time to build a credit score.

To improve your credit score, you must be able to repay a certain amount of debt over a period of time. This is a difficult and time-consuming process because many factors influence your credit score. Once you've established credit by taking out a loan, you'll start building your credit history and credit score as soon as you pay it back.

CHAPITRE 2:

Obtain Your Credit Report

It is simple to check your credit score online, but it can also be dangerous.

Hundreds of individual websites offer to check your credit quickly and often for free, but the process requires you to provide the sites with extremely personal information. Sensitive personal information such as your social security number, address, name, and, in some cases, a phone number are typically required. While these unofficial sites may be able to protect your credit score, they may sell your information and are generally untrustworthy.

Some of these websites are also concerned with identity theft. Due to potential security risks, you should never provide your full Social Security number online. While there are risks to obtaining your credit score online, there are ways to do so safely. One thing to keep in mind is that while most credit scoring websites now offer free credit score checks, others will try to charge you. This is a major red flag, and you should never pay for a credit check unless you absolutely need one.

Every year, you are required by law to check the top four lenders.

You can also view a denial report if your credit card bill was declined. The simplest but not the most convenient method is to contact each of the following credit bureaus: Experian, Equifax, Transunion, and Innovis. All of the websites of the agencies mentioned can be found with a simple search.

These agencies provide you with your credit score individually, but if you want to check your credit score quickly, you can always use one of the objective credit checkers, which combine scores from three, and sometimes four, agencies. www.experian.com is one of these sites. Sites such as Experian will also provide toll-free numbers for checking your credit score if you have any questions when providing information online.

Be aware, however, that all of the above agencies and websites will try to sell you packages and services aimed at creating, saving, or protecting your loan. While some of these services may be beneficial, the best way to build or protect your credit score is to spend and use credit responsibly.

It's never been easier to find out a person's credit score. Many online businesses today are centered on providing credit reporting services. Anyone who is interested can conduct an online search to find the best service for their specific needs.

It is true that an individual's creditworthiness is similar to a brand in many ways.

Many people and businesses will review this assessment and decide whether or not to partner with an individual based on it. However, many people are unaware that potential employers and colleges will also look through prospective employees' or students' records. A poor grade can cause a company or school to refuse to do business with that person.

The disadvantage of modern life is that a three-digit number can determine whether or not someone is worthy of association.

That is why knowing your credit score is so important. Knowledge is accompanied by the ability to apply that knowledge. If a person discovers that they have a low rating, they can take steps to improve their situation, such as debt consolidation or public debt grants and loans. In addition to a "good" result, there are ways to increase this number. In general, opening new credit accounts that a person can quickly pay off over time will boost their credit score.

BEWARE OF FREE CREDIT SCORE WEBSITES

Hundreds of websites provide free credit reports. The truth is, however, that many of these offers are not free. There are numerous tips and methods for duping you into parting with your hard-earned money.

The most popular websites provide a free credit report, but after filling out numerous online forms, you are asked to pay a fee. Many will pay for it because they spent a significant amount of time filling out all of the details and do not want to start over by finding another website or wasting more time.

Other methods exist, such as when they give access to your credit card information but then bill you a month later for a service you didn't notice in the fine print and have completely forgotten about.

Now that you know what to look out for, how can you find your credit score for free while avoiding all of the scam sites that seem to pop up everywhere?

While many businesses and websites provide a free credit report, only a few can be trusted.

Check Google to see how many websites there are. Before providing your information, read reviews or ask around. There are numerous ways to obtain credit score reports directly from institutions, so you don't need to rely on shady websites.

Even if you've chosen the right website, read the fine print for any additional services that may become available later.

HOW TO IMMEDIATELY IMPROVE YOUR CREDIT SCORE

There are numerous reasons why you may require a rapid increase in your credit score. One of them is that some employers have recently begun checking the credit scores of potential employees before hiring them. The reason for this is to ensure that employees can manage their finances and that financial difficulties do not affect their performance. If you are considering changing jobs but have bad credit, now is the time to consider taking steps to improve your credit. Don't put it off any longer.

The critical question now is how to effectively repair your bad credit. Let me walk you through some helpful steps:

Step 1: Determine your exact credit score.

Some people believe that because they haven't made multiple payments in the past, their credit scores are bad. This is incorrect. Before you take any further action, you must first determine your exact credit score. If you're in a hurry, you can check your credit score online at AnnualCreditReport.com.

To be safe, obtain a credit report from one of the major credit bureaus, such as Experian, TransUnion, or Equifax. Once you've determined your credit score, you'll need to devise a strategy to improve it. We would like to remind you to carefully review your credit report to ensure that there are no errors. If you notice an error on your credit report, contact your credit bureau right away to have it corrected.

Step 2: Gather funds to pay off your previous debts.

No matter how bad your credit report is, it would be beneficial if you faced it with courage at all times. If you have outstanding debts that you have not yet paid off, it is best to raise funds to pay them off.

Don't be afraid to contact debt collectors. Obtain their permission to remove negative entries from your report after you have paid your debts. If you are unable to pay off the debt in full, you can work with them to pay it off in installments. Never avoid debt collection agencies because doing so will harm your credit rating.

Step 3: Create a budget for paying your monthly bills.

You should keep an eye on your checking accounts in addition to managing your old debts. Your monthly payments must be made on time.

You can gradually improve your credit rating this way.

For example, if you have a credit card, you will be reminded to check your monthly statement to ensure there is no unpaid balance.

The truth is that no matter how bad your credit score appears to be right now, there are methods and strategies for improving it. Budgeting and debt repayment are the first steps.

Slowly and with the right information, you will gain a better understanding of the situation and be able to manage your finances with ease.

If you are unable to work with lenders to improve your credit score, it is best to seek the advice of a professional counselor who regularly deals with these issues.

It will help you improve your credit score after a few steps.

MORE ADVICE ON IMPROVING YOUR CREDIT SCORE

It is not difficult to obtain and maintain a high credit rating. At the very least, once you understand what it does, it will become simple, and you will wonder why you struggled with it for so long in the past. There are many things you must do to achieve a high score, and there are some things you must do to improve your score.

Let's look at what you can do right now to make the biggest difference.

Tip No. 1: Too Much Credit Is Bad!

If you've made the mistake of opening too many credit cards and lines of credit, you may be lowering your credit score without even realizing it.

Having a lot of credit available is great, but you never want to stretch yourself too thin and end up hurting yourself. It is not permitted to open more than 3 to 5 revolving accounts (credit card accounts) at the same time.

You should also save the balance on low-balance cards; the higher the balance, the less credit you have available, which will lower your credit score!

Tip 2 - Be cautious of who you give the opportunity to settle your loan with!

I made this mistake a few years ago when I authorized several car dealerships to handle my loans, and they all applied for sales cards within a few weeks. My rating was around 720, but it dropped to 680 when I removed all of the apps I had. My credit fell like a rock every time it was taken! Whatever the reason, credit bureaus do not like it when a loan is spent in a short period of time.

Tip 3 -Check Your Credit Report for Common Errors!

The majority of credit reports will contain some errors. Simply go through the report and look for anything that doesn't appear to be correct or is a separate error.

You will have the option to dispute and delete the records. This will significantly improve your credit score! Many people are unaware that mistakes are constantly present, but few people "make mistakes." Examine yours, or you might miss it!

THE EASY STEPS TO IMPROVING YOUR CREDIT WORTH

1. Pay your bills on time every time!

2. Live within your means!

3. Put money aside in a savings account for both small and large purchases. Please don't buy it if you don't need it! Save it if you want it!

4. Check your credit reports every six months for errors, inaccuracies, incorrect data, duplicates, and negative loans that are out of date. Once a year, you can get a FREE loan report online at annualcreditreport.com. If you want to check your credit reports more than once a year, you can buy them from each credit bureau for around $9.

The results will not change if you obtain your credit reports through your annual account or from one of the credit bureaus.

5. Keep your credit card balance to about one-third of your credit limit. Never exceed this amount, and never increase your credit card limit; doing so will result in lower credit scores.

Be aware that some credit card companies reduce consumption limits above maximum credit limits for no reason and without notice.

6. Open two or three revolving credit cards concurrently. Having too many revolving credit cards open, even if your balance is zero, indicates that you could increase your credit card limits tomorrow. If you are closing accounts, you should close new ones rather than old ones. You will have a higher credit score if you are older. Credit card companies honor the credit card account opening period. They typically demand at least a year or two of on-time payment.

7. If your driver's license has a license number, replace it with your usual computer-generated name. If you lose your driver's license, you have all the information necessary for someone to remove your credit identity. They can use your information to obtain credit, make online purchases, obtain credit cards, and so on.

If your Social Security number is removed from your driver's license, auto repair shops will be unable to run credit reports without your permission. For insurance purposes, some agents will request a driver's license. Nonetheless, they use your social security number, name, and address to run a credit report on you and determine whether you have enough credit before spending more time with you.

8. Call 1-888-303-7722 to unsubscribe from pre-approved spam.

9. Do not inadvertently apply for a loan or enter your social security number into forms. Loan applications appear on your credit report as inquiries, alerting lenders that you may be taking on new debt. Insurance companies now require your social security number in order to make you an offer. Don't apply for a loan on a regular basis (this is known as a hard move); your goal here is to keep your credit reports from displaying excessive demands, which will harm your credit score.

10. Lenders want to see consistency. It entails staying in the same place for more than two years, working in the same job/career for more than two years, and so on.

If you move frequently, get a mailbox to make it appear more stable.

11. If you have billing accounts, agree on a lower amount (this is referred to as debt settlement). This will save you money, but it does not mean the item will be removed from your credit report. A "paid collection" will be displayed, which is preferable to an "open collection." You can use credit repair to get derogatory items removed from your credit reports, whether they are paid or not. According to Section 611 of the Fair Credit Reporting Act, if an item on a credit report is inaccurate, out of date, duplicated, misleading, or cannot be verified, it must be removed or corrected.

According to the law, the consumer has the right to an accurate credit report. Given the number of errors the agency makes with people's credit reports, the statistics are staggering.

12. If collection agencies contact you, you should exercise your right under the Fair Debt Collection Practices Act and request that they "verify the debt." This will achieve four goals: 1. demonstrate that this unknown company has the legal right to collect the alleged debt; 2. demonstrate that an unnamed company proves that the debt is valid; 3. prevent them from making bothersome phone calls, and 4. prevent them from adding another negative tag to your credit report.

13. Any change in your credit report can have a significant impact on your results.

For example, simply closing two accounts reduces not only the number of accounts opened in slices (which usually improves your score) but also the total number of all open accounts (which usually lowers your score). Similarly, such action will affect the average age of all accounts, which may increase or decrease the count. As you can see, a single simple change has a significant impact on the number of items on your credit report. As a result, it is impossible to predict how a specific action will affect your credit score.

CHAPTER 3

The FICO Scoring Model

Most people are unaware that the credit bureau that issues your reports does not determine your credit score; instead, a third party called the Fair Isaac Corporation does (FICO).

They take into account all of the different aspects of your credit report to determine the number you receive. All of the information gathered by credit bureaus is combined to generate a three-digit number.

This is most likely the only grade you should be concerned about after you graduate from high school. It is the letter grade you receive for your financial stability. That single three-digit number will tell the rest of the world what they should think of you. However, it is more than just a number that reflects the present; it is also a path to your future. If there is an error in your reports, it is your responsibility to correct it. This is the most important and effective way to change it.

As a result, you must understand what is in your report in order to correct any incorrect or incomplete information. This will help you improve your score. There are very few people who have a perfect score, but you can improve yours if you know what to do.

FICO CREDIT SCORE COMPREHENDING

FICO Scores are a variety of factors that almost all lenders in the United States consider when making key credit decisions. According to a US News and World Report article, "the FICO Score is the most important piece of information in determining the amount you'll pay on a loan and whether you'll get credit." Such options include whether to endorse your credit application, what credit terms to offer you, and whether to increase your credit limit once your credit account has been established. FICO Scores are used by many creditors, including the top 50 lenders, making them the most widely used credit score. When you accept new credit and manage it tenaciously by reliably paying as agreed, you demonstrate to lenders that you don't have credit risk. Lenders use your credit history to determine how well you have managed your credit to date.

A FICO Score is a three-digit number calculated from the credit information on your credit report at a specific point in time at a customer reporting agency (CRA). It condenses the information on your credit report into a single number that lenders can use to assess your credit risk quickly, reliably, unbiasedly, and fairly.

Lenders will use your FICO Scores to assess your credit risk—and then approve your application. It is also an objective measure that you obtain based on your genuine purchasing and repayment history without being influenced by other types of information, such as race or religion.

Your FICO Scores from each agency may differ because FICO Scores are solely based on the credit information in that agency's credit file. Not all lenders report to all three CRAs.

Indeed, even when the lender reports to each of the three CRAs, the outcome may differ depending on the evaluation process.

Aside from the three-digit number, a FICO Score includes "score factors," which are the top factors that contribute to your score. Taking care of these score variables can help you improve your financial situation over time. Having a good FICO Score can put you in a better position to qualify for credit or better terms in the future.

Lenders use FICO Scores for a variety of credit items, including • Credit Cards • Auto Loans • Personal Loans & Lines of Credit • Student Loans • Home Equity Lines & Loans • Mortgages

FICO, or the Fair Isaac Company, calculates your credit score based on five factors:

History of Payment: a third of

Your credit history's length: 15%

Ten percent of credit was used.

10% of new credit is taken on.

Total Amount Owed to Lenders: 30 percent.

What exactly do these values imply? It means that certain factors will have a greater impact on your credit score. If you miss any payments or fail to make them on time, it will have a greater impact on your credit score than, say, the total amount of debt you have (Amount owed to lenders in total). Both of these factors are extremely important and should be taken very seriously. Your utilization is also included in the Total Amount you owe. This shows the amount of debt you have accumulated in comparison to your credit limit. If you use 30% or more of your credit limit, it will most likely have a negative impact on your credit score.

720 and Up Excellent

When you have this score, you are eligible for the best interest rates and repayment terms on all loans. This score can be useful if you plan to make large purchases. You will be able to obtain credit without difficulty and at the lowest possible interest rate. However, this score is extremely difficult to achieve. You will have to put in a lot of effort to keep this score up, and you will never get close to 800. The most you can hope for is to get close to 720 and stay there for as long as possible.

680-719-Good

When you fall into this category, you will receive good rates and terms, but not as good as those who have received excellent scores. With this score, you may be able to obtain favorable mortgage terms. You may not have as many problems, but you must be prepared to go from company to company to get your credit approved.

Again, this is not a common score. You'll need to put in extra effort to get it above 680.

If you are unable to cross this limit due to erroneous charges, you must make every effort to have them cleared as soon as possible.

620-679-Average

When you fall into this category, you can get reasonable mortgage terms and have it easier when purchasing smaller ticket items (though no better rate than good and excellent scores). Take care not to fall so low that a mortgage plan becomes unaffordable.

580-619-Poor

At this level, you can only get credit on the terms of the lenders. You will almost certainly have to pay more to obtain credit, so be prepared for additional fees. You should also keep in mind that if your credit score falls below this range, you will be unable to obtain auto financing, so you should work to improve it. This is where the vast majority of people fall.

Their score will be low primarily due to incorrect entries. If you are here, you will have a difficult time obtaining credit within your budget limits and will have to be prepared to pay a large sum of money.

500-579-Bad

If your credit score is in this range, you will pay a high price for credit. If you are looking for a 30-year mortgage, you may face interest rates that are 3% higher than what you would pay if you had good credit. On the other hand, if you want something for a short period of time, such as a 36-month auto loan, you will almost certainly pay nearly double the interest rate you would if you had good credit. So being here is most likely the worst thing that could happen to your credit report. It is nearly impossible to obtain low-interest rates.

Fewer than 500

If your credit score falls to this level, it may be nearly impossible to obtain any type of financing. If you do, the interest rate will be simply incomprehensible. You may have to work for 30 to 40 years to repay it. Your entire life will be devoted to repaying a loan that is unworthy of your time.

I'm sure a few of you fall into this category. But don't worry, help is on the way. If you fall into this category, you may be wondering if you can improve your score. The answer is yes! You can raise your credit score and potentially move into the good range.

WHERE DO THE OTHER THREE FACTORS FIT IN? WHAT ARE THE MEASUREMENTS?

To begin with, the longer you have credit, the better you will appear to the lender. The length of your credit history is determined by this.

Consider this to be relevant experience on your creditworthiness; the more you have, the higher your credit score will be. For this reason, a reasonable and sizable 15% of your credit score has been attached to your report.

Second, if you've recently applied for credit, it accounts for 10% of your overall score. Consider this recent relevant experience, but instead of a good job, you get good credit. The last thing credit companies consider when determining your credit score is the different types of credit you have.

A person's credit is likely to be slightly better than yours if they have a car loan and a mortgage on their credit report, in addition to credit cards, whereas yours only has credit card accounts.

HOW FICO SCORES CAN ASSIST YOU A FICO

Score provides lenders with a quick, objective, and predictable assessment of your credit risk. Prior to the use of scoring, the credit granting procedure could be moderate, conflicting, and unduly one-sided. Here are a few examples of how FICO Scores can help you.

Obtain credit more quickly

FICO Scores can be transmitted instantly, allowing lenders to expedite credit card and loan approvals. This implies that if you apply for credit, you will receive a response immediately, if not within seconds. Indeed, borrowers who score higher than the lender's minimum credit score can have their home loan application approved much faster. FICO Scores also enable retailers, websites, and other lenders to make "moment credit" decisions. Remember that FICO Scores are only one of many factors considered by lenders when making a credit decision.

Credit decisions are more appealing.

Using FICO Scores, lenders can focus on the facts associated with credit risk rather than their genuine beliefs or inclinations. FICO Scores, for example, do not take into account factors such as sexual orientation, race, religion, nationality, or marital status. When a lender uses your FICO Score, it is assessing your credit history in a reasonable and objective manner.

A higher FICO score saves you money.

When you apply for credit – whether it's a credit card, a vehicle loan, an individual loan, or a home loan – lenders need to know how risky you are as a borrower in order to determine an appropriate amount. Your FICO Scores may influence not only whether or not a lender grants you credit but also how much and at what interest rate.

Consider the following two models:

On a 30-year contract, two people will receive $230,000 each. A borrower with a FICO score of 760 may pay $211 less in interest per month than a borrower with a FICO score of 630. That equates to $75,960 in investment funds over the life of the loan.

On a $20,000, 48-month auto loan, a borrower with a FICO Score of 720 could pay $131 less in interest per month than a borrower with a FICO Score of 580. This amounts to a total of $6,288 over the term of the loan.

Many people are unaware that it is a federal law that requires you to review your credit reports at least once a year. It may appear strange, but there was a time when you would not have been permitted to see what information had been gathered about you. Because you would not have been their primary consumer, the credit bureaus felt they were not required to notify you of any information gathered about you. However, a federal law enacted about 25 years ago changed everything. You can now check each of these agencies' reports at least once a year.

If you haven't checked your report in a long time, it's a good idea to do so now. If you have checked it, it is recommended that you pull from a single agency once every four months to see what has changed on your report and make corrections as soon as they occur. Obtaining a copy is simple. To begin, go to AnnualCreditReport.com and follow the on-screen instructions to request your report.

CHAPTER 4

The Distinction between FICO and Other Credit Scores

DIFFERENT BUREAUS APPLICATIONS DIFFERENT CREDIT SCORE CALCULATION MODELS

There are various scores that lenders can obtain from the various bureaus, and the score for one may not mean the same thing as the score for the other. This is significant because when you receive your credit score, it is critical that you understand exactly what your number means and whether you are in hot water or not.

Different lenders have different credit scoring ranges. Here are some of the most popular:

a) FICO Credit Scoring Range Expansion:

The credit score range is 350-850. Many lenders look at your credit report and see the Fair Isaac Corporation's credit score.

This is one of the most commonly used scores. The FICO score indicates your creditworthiness in the eyes of lenders.

There is no longer just one type of FICO score, as new NextGen scores with a range of up to 950 have been introduced.

b) Vantage Score Credit Scoring Range Expansion:

501-990. The Vantage Score credit scoring model is comprised of three major credit bureaus: TransUnion, Equifax, and Experian.

This Vantage Score will most likely be provided to you when you receive your credit score directly from one of these bureaus. It is also known as the Vantage Score 2.0 model.

c) Vantage Scores 3.0 Credit Scoring Range Expansion:

300-850 This credit scoring model is very similar to the one before it (Vantage Score 2.0 Model). The only significant difference is that the Vantage Score 3.0 Range has a slightly larger range, i.e., 300-850.

d) Expansion of the Trans Risk Credit Scoring Range:

300-850. This range is used by the credit bureau Trans Union when attempting to determine your creditworthiness.

e) Equifax Credit Scoring Range Extender:

280-850 This is the scoring range used by credit bureau Equifax to determine how risky lending to you is.

f) Experian Plus Credit Scoring Range Expansion:

330-830 This one is used by the credit bureau Experian and is how the credit bureau determines your creditworthiness.

THE DISTINCTION BETWEEN FICO AND OTHER CREDIT SCORES

Another question you may have is the distinction between the FICO score and the other credit scores. To begin, these are the only ones created by the Fair Isaac Corporation, and they are used by approximately 90% of the top lenders when making overall lending decisions.

This is because FICO scores will be regarded as the gold standard for making fair and accurate decisions about an individual's creditworthiness.

There are now other credit scores available, and they can be used in certain situations. These other scores will calculate the number they provide you within a different way than the FICO score. So, while some of those other scores may appear to be similar to the FICO score, they aren't. Only FICO scores will be used by the majority of the top lenders you want to borrow from, and while the others can be useful for some monitoring of your score, if you want, the FICO score is the best way to go.

CHAPTER 5

What Is the Importance of Having a Good Credit Score?

When you apply for credit, insurance, phone service, or even a place to live, providers want to know if you are low risk. And they use credit scores to make that decision.

A credit score is simply a number. A high score indicates that you have good credit. A low score indicates that you have poor credit.

A higher score indicates that you are lower risk and are more likely to obtain the product or service - or pay less for it.

It works like this: Credit managers pull information from your credit reports, such as your payment history, account age, unpaid debts, and collection actions that were taken against you.

Credit scores can be applied in a variety of ways. Here are a few examples.

1. Insurance companies use the information in your credit report, combined with other factors, to predict the likelihood that you will present an insurance claim and the amount you may be able to claim. They use this information to determine whether or not to provide you with insurance and how much you will be charged.

2. Credit scores are used by public service providers to determine whether a new customer deposit is required to provide the service. Scores are also used by cell phone providers and homeowners who rent out their homes when considering a new client or tenant.

Each type of company has its own scoring system, and credit scoring models can be based on information other than your credit report data.

When you apply for a mortgage loan, for example, the system can take into account the amount of the advance, the total amount of your debts, and your income.

EASY ACCESS TO THE BEST CREDIT CARDS

A good credit score is required to be eligible for a credit card that offers excellent cash-back reward programs, amazing benefits, low rates, and many other benefits. Aside from paying lower interest and fees, having access to the best credit card allows you to obtain a higher credit limit. As a result, you can have the freedom and flexibility to make the purchases you want without the financial constraints that come with a low credit limit.

An increase in your credit limit increases your creditworthiness over time. This demonstrates to banks and other lending institutions that you are mature enough and capable of handling the responsibilities that come with having access to a large amount of credit.

A good credit score can help you find cards with cash-back rates as high as 5% at various locations such as restaurants, grocery stores, ecommerce platforms, gas stations, and any other time your card is used.

EASY LOAN ACCESS

Because you are afraid of being turned down if you have a bad credit history, you will be hesitant to apply for a new credit card or loan. Maintaining a good credit score reveals a lot about your creditworthiness. When banks and lending institutions see your credit score, they can be confident that they are not at risk and that you will repay the money you are asking them to lend you. Though this does not guarantee approval because other factors such as your income, debts, and so on are also taken into account, it does provide you with a very good chance of getting approval.

LOWER LOAN INTEREST RATES

Your interest rate is directly proportional to your credit score. Assume you have an excellent credit score. In that case, you may not need to consider the interest rate when applying for a credit card because you will always qualify for the lowest interest rates, resulting in very low credit card loan charges. You must have a good credit score if you want to always have a low-interest rate.

EASY APPROVAL FOR HOUSING AND APARTMENT RENTAL

Many landlords and apartment owners check credit scores for the same reason that lenders do on a regular basis. They are concerned that tenants with poor credit will be unable to pay their rent on time, so they avoid tenants who pose a high risk.

Having previous bad credit scores gives the property owner the impression that you might not be able to pay back on time, whereas a good credit score says otherwise.

IMPROVED JOB APPLICATIONS

Although this is not the only criterion considered by employers, many employers check the credit histories of various job applicants during the application process, especially if the job you're applying for requires handling money or accessing sensitive financial information from clients.

The majority of employers believe that your ability to use credit responsibly makes you a more likely employee.

POWER IN NEGOTIATION

If you have a good credit score, you can use it to negotiate a lower interest rate on your student loan, new credit card, mortgage, and other loans.

Having a credit card with a clean history gives you more bargaining power, which is necessary to secure the favorable terms that you require. As a result, you can carefully select the terms that will be of great benefit to your current financial situation.

CHAPTER 6

What Factors Influence My Score?

PAYING LATE OR NOT PAYING AT ALL

Paying late on anything is one of the worst things you can do for your credit score. About 35% of your score will be based on your payment history, so if you are not on time, your score will suffer greatly. Being late on these payments on a regular basis will do a lot of damage to your credit score. Pay your bills on time, especially credit card bills.

Worse than paying late is failing to pay at all. If you decide to completely disregard your credit cards and other bills and do not pay them at all, you will be in even more trouble. Each month that you fail to make a credit card payment, you will be one month closer to having your account charged off.

If you want to improve your credit score, especially if you want to get it up to 800 or higher, you must stop making late payments. This is a bad thing because it shows that you are unwilling to pay back your money, and they are less likely to give you more money as a result.

If you're having trouble making payments, whether they're frequently late or don't come in at all, it's time to create a budget.

You live above your means, which is never a good sign of improving your credit score. When you establish a budget and begin paying your debts on time, you will be able to raise your credit score in no time.

ACCOUNTS BEING CHARGED-OFF OR SENT TO COLLECTIONS

The next step is to have your accounts charged off. When creditors are concerned that you will not pay your bills for loans or credit cards, they will charge off your accounts.

A charge-off indicates that the insurer has given up hope of ever hearing from you again. This does not mean that you will no longer be held accountable for the debt. When it comes to your credit score, this is one of the absolute worst things you can do.

Another problem arises when one of your accounts is sent to collections.

Creditors frequently collaborate with debt collectors in order to collect payments. Collectors may send your account to collections after, but sometimes before, charging it off completely. Even if the account is charged off at the time, this is never a good thing. If your bills are going to collections or being charged off, it means that you haven't just missed one or two payments. It means that you have gone so long without paying the entire amount that the company believes you will never pay it back. Either they have written it off as a tax deduction, or they have sold it to a credit collection company that will harass you in the future.

This is almost never a good thing. You will be harassed for a long time in order to repay your debt. It will demonstrate to other creditors that you have not simply missed a few payments when times are tough.

It demonstrates to them that you fell so far behind that someone else, someone who had previously given you money, decided to abandon you in the process. This is difficult to combat and will not persuade a new creditor to lend you the money you require.

BANKRUPTCY APPLICATION

This is a bit extreme and should be avoided at all costs. Bankruptcy is an extreme measure that will devastate the credit score that you are working with. It will also appear on your record for seven to ten years. Before filing for bankruptcy, it is a good idea to consult with an advisor about all of your options.

You must do everything in your power to avoid bankruptcy at all costs. It may appear to be the best option to work with. When you declare bankruptcy, you believe that you can simply walk away from all of your debts and never have to worry about them again. However, this is not how the entire process is going to work for you.

There are various types of bankruptcies that you can use, but you will almost always need to go through the process and pay off as much of the debt as possible.

And, in some cases, it can take years of making payments and having your wages confiscated and taken away before you can even file for bankruptcy. You could simply pay the debts for that period of time instead, or reach an agreement with the creditors for a lower amount if necessary, and now have the stigma of bankruptcy on your side.

When the bankruptcy is finished, which can take some time, a new problem will arise. For a long time, you must concentrate on how you will deal with the black mark on your credit report. This could take anywhere between seven and ten years. And you can bet that creditors will not be pleased with all of that. For a long time afterward, you will find it difficult to obtain credit or other forms of financial assistance. To avoid bankruptcy, you must learn how to work with a budget and figure out the best ways to manage your money, regardless of your income level. This is easier to manage than you might think, and it can help you get on a good payment schedule to deal with your debts and pay them off. Bankruptcy appears to be a simple way out of debt. It continues to haunt you for many years afterward. It may make obtaining credit in the future difficult, and it will not address the underlying issue that has landed you in this situation.

CLOSING AN EXISTING CREDIT ACCOUNT

It has been observed that closing old credit accounts lowers one's credit score, particularly if the card has a balance. One of the factors used to calculate your credit scores is the age of your credit history.

Closing an old account will cause the average age of your account to drop, thereby reducing the overall credit age you have available on your credit accounts. This reduces your credit usage and may harm your credit score.

MAKING A NEW LOAN OR CREDIT APPLICATION

When you apply for a loan, the financial institution will almost certainly conduct a "credit application search" on your credit report, which must be authorized by you before a decision is made whether or not to lend you money.

This credit application search may have a minor impact on your credit score. When you make multiple requests in a short period of time, the damage to your account becomes enormous.

To avoid drops in your credit score from frequent checks, make sure you are in desperate need of funds before applying for credit.

FRAUDULENT FINANCIAL SETTLEMENTS

Declaring yourself legally bankrupt has serious consequences for your credit score and can significantly harm it. Other derogatory financial settlements, such as tax evasions and civil judgments, among others, could harm your credit score.

These items demonstrate that you are unable to properly manage your finances and that you are a risky individual to lend money to.

CARDS WITH HIGH BALANCES OR MAXED OUT CARDS

You should always keep an eye on your credit card balances. The second most important aspect of our credit score is the amount of debt we have on them, which is measured by credit utilization. Having high credit card balances in comparison to your credit limit will increase credit utilization and lower your credit score. For example, if you have a $10,000 credit limit on a card but the balance is $9500 or higher, your score will not reflect this.

You should also make certain that you are not maxing out or exceeding the credit card limit. Credit cards that are over the limit or maxed out will result in a credit utilization of 100 percent.

This is one of the most detrimental things you can do to your credit score. Make an effort to pay down your debts as quickly as possible in order to maintain your credit score and keep it from plummeting.

CANCELLATION OF CREDIT CARDS

There are several ways that closing your card will result in a drop in your credit score. First, consider closing a card that is still in good standing. When you close that card, your credit limit will be reduced to $0, but your balance will remain unchanged. This will make it appear as if you have maxed out the credit card, which will lower your credit score slightly. If you want to close your account, make sure you pay off the balance before you do so.

Another thing to think about is what will happen if you close your old credit cards. The length of your credit history will account for approximately 15% of your credit score, with longer credit histories being preferable. Closing old cards, especially the oldest ones, will make your history appear much shorter than it is. Even if you no longer use the card and there are no annual fees, you should keep it open because you are losing nothing and gaining more.

Finally, we must exercise caution when closing cards with available credit. If you have more than one credit card to work with, some with balances and some without, closing the cards with no balances will increase your credit utilization. You can simply keep those out of the way and watch your credit score improve.

INSUFFICIENT MIX ON THE REPORT

While this is not as important as some of the other options, having a good mix of credit will account for about 10% of your credit score at the time. If you have a report with only one or two items on it, such as credit cards or loans, it is likely that the score you are working with will be impacted in some way.

The more you can mix up your accounts and fill them with a variety of items, the better. You don't want to overextend yourself, but having a mix of loans, mortgages, credit cards, and other debts that you pay off on time each month is one of the best ways to improve your credit score without causing harm or paying too much in the process.

This does not imply that you should go out and apply for multiple jobs at the same time in order to get your mix-up. This is a common occurrence; naturally, the longer you work on improving your credit score, the more likely it is. You might have a few credit cards, and then you get a car loan and pay it off. Maybe you need a loan for a vacation or home improvement, so you'll open those accounts first and then apply for a mortgage.

These various loans and credit amounts will come and go over time, but they will all appear in your credit mix and help raise your score. If you try to increase your mix all at once, you will raise some red flags against your credit, which can also cause problems. Doing this over a few years is the most effective way to ensure that your credit score rises.

APPLYING FOR TOO MANY POSITIONS

Credit inquiries are another factor that will be included in your report.

These will account for about 10% of the total score you work with.

You are making multiple loans and credit applications in a short period of time will result in a significant drop in your credit score. Always keep credit applications to a minimum so that you are not harmed along the way.

In some cases, this will not have a significant impact on you. For example, if you have good credit and want to apply for a mortgage, you should apply for several mortgages and shop around a bit. If you do these close together, it will not be seen as a negative because the lender will assume this is what you are doing rather than you taking on too much or being turned down. If they ask, you can easily explain this to them. In most other cases, however, this is not a good sign. Having all of those inquiries on your score will lower it slightly, at least in the short term.

When other lenders notice that you're applying for a lot of credit, they'll assume you're getting turned down. They will be perplexed as to why, or they will assume that you are taking on too much credit that you will be unable to manage, and they will refuse to lend you any money. These are just a few of the various things you will have to deal with when it comes to dealing with your credit report. Sometimes the things that can hurt your score are far more important than the things that can help you improve your score. Working on both will be important when it comes down to it, and knowing how to avoid some of the common mistakes that can ruin your credit in no time is critical to raising your score and seeing it work the way you want it to.

CHAPTER 7

Commitment, Discipline, and a Positive Attitude Will Make a Difference!

AVOIDING BAD CREDIT WITH THE RIGHT MINDSET

A financial mindset is an overarching mentality that you have about your finances. It has an impact on how you make important financial decisions every day.

It will have a significant impact on your ability to achieve your objectives. When you change your perspective on money, you'll be able to make better decisions about how to solve problems.

Constructive thought has an effect in this situation.

CHARACTERISTICS OF A BAD MONEY MINDSET

Your attitude toward money is similar to moral fatigue in that it motivates you to act.

If you have a positive attitude toward money, you are more likely to be confident and take the necessary steps to be effective.

Negativity, on the other hand, generates emotions that prevent action:

Intimidation or fear

Defeatism

Procrastination

It becomes more difficult to see the way forward as you change your attitude toward money and focus on the benefits of what you should achieve.

A new perspective on money will make it easier to achieve your objectives. So, how do you cultivate a positive attitude toward money?

A POSITIVE MONEY MINDSET'S QUALITIES

When you accept financial positivity, you realize that no problem is insurmountable. This will be done regardless of whether you have $5,000 or $50,000 in interest. Even if your credit score is 500, no loan limit will last forever.

When you have a positive attitude toward your finances, you begin to look for opportunities rather than obstacles, and you realize that any financial problem is solvable.

The key to success is to resolve negative emotions and focus on the positive.

APPLYING A POSITIVE MONEY MINDSET TO OVERCOME FINANCIAL DIFFICULTIES

Positivity can be difficult to cultivate when you are in a stressful situation, but it is essential.

Assume you have a credit card debt of more than $50,000. Your negativity is most likely caused by a combination of factors, including:

• The total monthly contributions are approximately $1,250, and the budget is close • However, despite spending too much, the balances never seem to drop

High-interest rates currently account for approximately 60% of every investment you make • As a result, adhering to the minimum contributions would take more than 40 years to recover everything you owe

The first step toward debt repayment and changing your financial habits is to change your perspective on income. By imagining what a debt-free life would be like, gaining financial security, and having the freedom to spend your money on the things you enjoy the most, staying focused and meeting your financial goals becomes much easier.

Your strategic focus should be on finding alternatives. You are not the first person to fall into debt so quickly. Begin with what you know: Minimal payments will not have a significant impact, so you must devise a better strategy. The situation changes dramatically if you simply repay the bills at $1,250 rather than meeting the full payment plan. The payout deadline will be met in 62 months rather than 502 months. In reality, five years is a reasonable length of time for a debt repayment strategy.

ACHIEVE FINANCIAL BALANCE

A positive financial mindset is comprised of more than just attitude. You, too, require harmony. Stability promotes harmony in your financial life.

When you devote all of your energy to debt repayment, you won't have any money available in the event of a disaster. Or, if you spend the entire day today focusing on the schedule, you won't be able to properly save for retirement.

A money mantra keeps a financial goal in the forefront of your mind, making it easier to take the steps necessary to achieve your desired results. Now, let's look at how to create a great personal finance mantra.

A MONEY MOTIVATION

A money motto is a clear statement of what you intend to do with your money. This can either encourage you to make sound financial decisions or discourage you from making poor ones. Its purpose is to remind you and give you confidence in your daily life.

You state what you want to manifest, and you are encouraged to act by simply thinking about it. Begin by daydreaming about a specific financial goal you want to achieve in the next six months.

THE SNOWBALL METHOD FOR DEBT

The debt snowball approach is a debt management technique in which you pay off the debt in proportion to the amount owed, gaining traction as each balance is paid off. When the smallest loan is paid off in full, the interest you owe will be transferred to the next smallest balance.

It functions as follows:

Step I

Sort your debts by interest rate, starting with the smallest and working your way up.

Step II

Make minimum payments on all of your debts except the smallest ones.

Step III

Pay as much as you can on your smallest debt.

Step IV

Continue until all debts have been paid in full.

The Debt Snowball is depicted.

Assume you have four debts:

$500 medical bill – $50 payment

Payment for a $2,500 credit card debt is $63 per month.

$7,000 car loan—$135 monthly payment

$10,000 student loan—$96 monthly payment

Following the debt reduction method, you will make small payments on everything except the hospital bill. But suppose you get an extra $500 per month because you've taken on a side job to keep your expenses to a bare minimum. If you spend $550 per month on the hospital bill (the cost of $50 plus the remaining $500), the interest will be waived in one month. You would then use the $550 freed up the following month to pay off the credit card balance, charging a total of $613 ($550 plus the minimum amount of $63). You'll be able to get rid of your credit card in four months if you do it this way. You make it worthwhile!

Now, hit the auto loan for $748 per month in the nose. Within ten months, it will vanish into the sunset. You're all on the right track! By the time you reach the student loan, which is the main liability, you will have added $844 per month to it. That means it will also be paid in about 12 months.

Your decisions today will have an impact on tomorrow. Make yourself wise as well.

CHAPTER 8

Can I Improve My Score to 800 or More Points?

Now comes the difficult part. Maybe you've been doing some of the work we go over in this guidebook, and you've noticed a significant increase in the amount of your FICO score.

This is always good news, but we'd like to see if we can raise our score to 800 or higher. This is a score reserved for the elite. It is difficult to obtain because it necessitates, among other things, a perfect balance of credit types, a high credit limit, and no missed payments. However, it is possible.

When you can raise your credit score to this level, it will be much easier for you to obtain credit and loans whenever you want. If something happens and you have a lot of medical bills to pay, this credit score can help you out. It can also be used for non-emergencies, such as starting a business, buying a new house, or doing something else along those lines.

So, how do you ensure that you can raise your credit score to 800 or higher? The first step is to understand the facts. Once you have answered the main question of "What is a perfect credit score?" you will find it easier to take the necessary steps to determine exactly what you can do to achieve the perfect score. But first, you should determine where you fall on the FICO scale.

You can get a free annual credit report from any of the country's three major credit bureaus once a year. If you go through this and find any problems with any of them (sometimes a mistake will appear on one but not the others), now is the time to fix them. If your report contains numerous errors, you will never achieve an 800+ score.

The next thing you can concentrate on is establishing a long credit history.

With a few exceptions, lenders will generally view borrowers with short credit histories as riskier to work with. To achieve a credit score of 800 or higher, you must first establish and then maintain a long history. Even if you don't use some of the accounts, keeping them open will help you improve your score.

As previously stated, you must ensure that all of your bills are paid on time. There isn't a single person with a credit score of 800 or higher who doesn't have a missed payment, or a series of missed payments, on their report. Paying your bills late or not paying them at all will lower your credit score. If you have trouble remembering due dates, consider enrolling in automatic payments to have that taken care of for you.

You should also take the time to rethink your credit card usage. The utilization rate for your credit, which is the amount of debt you owe divided by the total credit available, will account for approximately 30% of your score. Typically, we want to stay under 30%, but if you want to get a higher score, staying under 10% is best.

One thing we haven't covered much in this guidebook yet that will help you get the higher score you want is learning how to diversify the accounts you have.

This is one of the best ways to strengthen your credit, and while it may take some time, you will find it is a great way for us to ensure your credit score can rise.

When you are able to diversify your accounts, you can improve your credit score. This is not an excuse to go out and open ten different credit card accounts at the same time. This means you should have a variety of credit, such as an auto loan, a student loan, a mortgage, and a credit card. Ten credit cards will not result in a diverse mix of debt or demonstrate responsibility with your credit score. However, having a variety of accounts, even if some of them are paid off, is going to be a much better option to work with.

While you work on improving your credit score, make sure you cut your spending and create a budget that you can stick to. This allows you to stay within your means and reduces the likelihood that you will go overboard with your spending. Although your income will not be considered when calculating your credit score, living within your means, whatever that number is, is a great way to improve your score.

The next item on your to-do list is to figure out how to limit the liability you're dealing with. When you go to cosign a loan, keep in mind that while it may appear to be a nice thing to do, you are actually taking a risk for someone else.

If you do this for someone who is unable to manage their debt well, it will have a negative impact on your credit because you will be responsible for that debt as well. If you want to ensure that you can obtain and maintain a credit score of 800 or higher, you should avoid cosigning at all costs.

In addition, you should make certain that your liability is limited in other ways. Cards that have been lost or stolen should always be reported as soon as possible. If you do not do this, you will most likely be held liable for any purchases that were not authorized at the time.

And if you are unable to make those purchases, your credit score will suffer as a result.

Finally, you must ensure that you are restricting the difficult inquiries that occur in your report. You are dealing with an inquiry, whether it is you or another agency or institution pulling out the credit report and asking for a copy of it. A soft inquiry may occur on occasion, but it is unlikely to result in any changes to your credit.

This soft inquiry will take place if one of the following events occurs:

You go through your credit report and check it.

You authorize an employer with whom you may work in the future to check your credit.

You have your credit checked by the financial institutions with which you do business.

You receive a credit card offer that has been preapproved, and the company checks your credit.

While a soft inquiry will not have a significant impact on your credit scores, a hard inquiry should be avoided. This is the one that can have an impact on your credit score. When a company pulls your credit report after you apply for a product such as a credit card or a mortgage, this is referred to as a credit inquiry. You want to make sure that you can limit the difficult inquiries as much as possible in order to achieve the best results with this.

CHAPTER 9

How to Improve Your Credit Score by 100+ Points in 30-60 Days

Building your credit can be an agonizingly slow process at times, but there are a few simple steps you can take to improve your score in as little as a month or two, as discussed in the following sections.

PAY OFF YOUR CREDIT LINES AND CREDIT CARDS.

Lowering your debt use proportion, the difference between the amounts of revolving credit that are available to you and the amount that you're utilizing is probably the quickest way to support a score. One simple way to improve your proportion is to redistribute your debt. If you have a large balance on one card, for example, you could transfer a portion of the debt to another card. It's usually better for your credit scores to have small balances on several cards rather than a large balance on a single card.

LIGHTLY USE YOUR CREDIT CARDS

The scoring formula prefers a significant difference between your balances and your limits, and it doesn't care whether you pay off your balances in full each month or carry them from month to month. What matters is how much of your credit limit you're actually using at any given time. You can boost your score by paying off the card completely a few days before the deadline.

For example, if your bills are usually mailed on the 25th, you can check your balance online about seven days beforehand and pay off whatever is owed, plus extra to cover charges that may appear before the 25th.

When the bills are actually printed, their balances are nearly zero.

(If you use this method, make sure to make a second payment after your announcement appears if your balance isn't already zero.)

This will protect you from being harmed by late fees, which can occur even if you made a payment before the end of the month.)

WORK ON CORRECTING THE MAJOR MISTAKES IN YOUR CREDIT REPORTS.

If another person's bankruptcy, collections, or charge-offs appear on your report, you must work to have them removed.

If an account you closed is still listed as open, you'll need to correct it. Having an account marked as "closed" on your file will not help your score and will actually harm it.

USE THE BUREAUS ONLINE DISPUTE RESOLUTION PROCESS

Some claim that using the online dispute process yields faster results.

In any case, you'll need to print out all of your correspondence and anything else you've sent out.

CHECK TO SEE IF YOU CAN HAVE YOUR CREDITORS UPDATE POSITIVE ACCOUNTS OR REPORT ON THEM.

Not all creditors report to all three bureaus, and some do not report consistently. If you can persuade a creditor to report a good-standing account, you may see a quick drop in your credit score.

CHECK YOUR CREDIT REPORT FOR ANY ERRORS.

You may be wondering what the distinction between a credit score and a credit report is. A credit report, on the other hand, is a document that contains all of the information used to calculate your credit score. Having said that, there is always the possibility of an error when calculating your score. It is well known that approximately 21% of people have errors on at least one of their reports. This means that nearly a quarter of people with credit scores have a lower score as a result of errors.

DOUBLE-CHECK YOUR ERRORS

If you want to dispute an item, you must write to the credit reporting agency and inform them that you want to dispute an item, or more than one item, found on your credit report. It is critical that you include the reason for your disagreement.

Once completed, your request should be sent in the form of a letter via certified mail. It's also a good idea to ask for a return receipt. This ensures that your dispute has been received by the credit agency in question. Make sure you keep copies of any letters you send, as well as any attachments. This obligates the credit reporting agency to investigate and determine whether your dispute is valid. This usually happens over the course of 30 days.

SET UP AUTO-PAY ON YOUR CREDIT CARDS

It doesn't matter if you use a physical calendar taped to your wall or an app on your smartphone to set an alert; you should do whatever you can to be reminded when credit card payments are due. Ensure that you consistently pay more than the minimum. When you consider that your payment history and the size of your debt are the two most important determinants of your credit score, it makes sense to pay as much as you can towards your debt.

CHAPTER 10

How to Build a Credit Score From the Ground Up?

There are several options, all of which are effective.

THE FIRST STEP IS TO OPEN A BANKING ACCOUNT.

Having an account open will not improve your score, but it will provide you with a starting point for demonstrating consistent income. After a few months, you can ask your bank (while wearing your best smile) what services they provide to help you improve your credit score. My bank, for example, offers a $ 500 tiered loan that must be returned in 6 months.

It means that you deposit $500, they re-loan it to you at a low-interest rate, and when you finish paying the installments in 6 months, they return the $500. In essence, you paid interest as a "tax" for the sole purpose of accumulating points in 6 months. To put it another way, you return 500 and 500, then pay 500 in installments + interest, and return 500 at the end. It is an expense, but this type of loan guarantees you a significant accumulation of points, but only if you make your payments on time.

THE SECOND STEP IS TO REQUEST A SECURED CREDIT CARD.

Unlike traditional credit cards, you do not need to show any type of entry to be approved, but there is a usage limit. The only requirement is a deposit, which is refunded after a year of regular use. Until a few years ago, the deposit was around 200 euros, but due to the debt problems that arose following the recession, all of the major credit companies have reduced the costs. For example, I applied with Capital One (but there are numerous other options, such as Discover). The deposit was only $ 49, and the card's monthly limit was $ 200, with the option of 2% cash back on gas or restaurant purchases. I began using it on a monthly basis ONLY for these two purposes, and after a year, my credit score was considered very good; they also returned the deposit and cash, and the credit limit was increased to $500 after only six months. Of course, you are not required to use it exclusively for these purposes, but I have restricted myself for two reasons.

The first is to save money (i.e., get a refund) at the end of the year.

The second is to ensure that I never use more than 30% of the card limit.

That brings me to my next point.

NEVER EXCEED 30% OF THE CREDIT CARD LIMIT.

Believe it or not, it is critical that you demonstrate that you do not require a credit card to pay for your purchases and that you only use it when absolutely necessary or as an optional choice.

The more you use it, the better, but use it sparingly.

PAY YOUR INSTALLMENTS ON TIME.

All of the preceding points are meaningless if you are not consistent with your payments. Nobody here deducts your loan or credit card debts from your paycheck. It is your responsibility to remember to pay or to set up an automatic payment from your bank account. I made the decision to set up automatic payments.

Even if you have a great memory, you never know what can happen to distract you and cause you to forget the due date. So I strongly advise you to do the same because even one late payment will have a negative impact on your credit score.

CHANGE THE TYPES OF DEBT AS MUCH AS POSSIBLE.

If you can get the Secured Card and the mini loan from the bank at the same time, go ahead and do it. The greater your options, the faster your credit score will rise. Of course, if you don't pay on time, the opposite effect will occur, and your credit score will plummet before it has even had a chance to grow. So, if you're not confident that you can do better, don't take the risk and wait a little longer.

ADD YOUR NAME AS AN "AUTHORIZED USER" TO SOMEONE ELSE'S CREDIT CARD.

If, for example, you are married to an American who has had more time than you to build a good credit score (as in my case), he should make you an authorized user on his credit cards. This does not imply that you will be forced to use his credit cards, but the better his credit score, the better his influence on yours. But be cautious! If you fall, he will follow you. This type of decision requires a significant amount of trust, so be careful not to betray it.

GET THE FREE CREDIT KARMA APP

It not only provides you with a detailed report of your score on a regular basis, but also what has positively or negatively influenced it, which credit cards or loans are best suited to your

situation, your progress, and a variety of other functions.

It's all free and, while not up to the minute, fairly accurate. It does not affect your credit score and also provides you with a variety of other services such as online and free tax returns. Because of Credit Karma, other major credit companies have had to adapt in order to provide a free credit score check.

Capital One and Discover, for example, have now incorporated this service into their offerings (although in a more limited way).

If you follow these tips for a year, you will be able to obtain a car loan without paying disproportionate interest or even more, depending on your income and general receivables/payables situation. This reminds me of how critical it is to get started as soon as possible. Keep in mind that this is the first thing they look at when you apply for a loan!

HOW TO IMPROVE YOUR CREDIT SCORE OVER TIME

Once you've started to work your way out of a bad credit situation, the most important factor becomes increasing your score. Making your payments on time is, of course, a great way to balance your previously negative activity, but there are other, more creative ways to achieve the same result.

Let's take a look at how you can improve your credit in the eyes of a lender.

Resolve any outstanding balances

Assume you have a debt that was eventually turned over to a collection agency because you refused to pay it back on time.

Of course, the debt you owe will appear as a negative on your credit report, but if a collection agency is involved, you have the opportunity to influence how this debt is perceived.

Negotiation skills are required

You appear responsible if you go to a collection agency and negotiate a deal in which you only pay a portion of your debt rather than the entire amount. Furthermore, your credit report will show that your outstanding debt has been settled, which will help to improve your credit score. Other suggestions include putting the agreement in writing and specifying how much you are willing to pay.

Twice a month, pay your bills.

Assume you've had a particularly difficult month in terms of unexpected bills and expenses. As a result, you've decided to spend close to your credit limit to make up for it. Your credit limit is four thousand dollars, and you have already spent three thousand this month. This is not the worst situation for you because you know you have the funds and intend to pay off your entire debt by the end of the month.

Instead, consider making several payments throughout the month. You will be able to reduce the amount of debt that the credit card company sees this way. It will appear that you simply reallocated your funds in a specific way rather than that you are maxing out a card and are experiencing financial difficulties.

This strategy should be considered, especially if you have other credit cards that are close to being maxed out or are completely maxed out.

Boost Your Credit Limit

If you are unable to pay down high outstanding balances on your credit cards at this time, another viable option is to request an increase in your credit limit. This could be an excellent option for you, especially if you have recently received a raise. As previously discussed, having low utilization is critical to maintaining a good credit score. By extending more credit to yourself, it appears that you are using less credit than is currently available to you. While this will help you build your credit, it can be risky if your spending habits are less than conservative.

You must ensure that you will not immediately spend more of your credit once it has been extended to you by the credit company. If you suspect that this is the result of a credit extension, consider one of the other options presented in this chapter. Similar to a gambling addiction, it may appear that spending credit card money creates a rush because the need to repay the funds is not immediate. If you find it difficult to resist the urge to spend large sums of money on your credit card, you may have a credit card addiction.

If you notice that you are frequently maxing out your credit card on frivolous or unnecessary purchases, you may need to seek assistance.

Even if you don't consider yourself a total credit card addict, seeking financial counseling may help you save money. Saving money can also help you improve your credit score because it is money that is not being spent in ways that cannot be repaid. To put it another way, learning to be financially responsible will help you build your credit. Hiring a financial advisor can assist you in learning what to save and how to save it, as well as learning how to properly manage your funds.

Chapter 11

How to Improve Your Credit Score

Following Foreclosure and Bankruptcy

MANAGEMENT OF FORECLOSURES, BANKRUPTCY, TAX LIENS, AND OTHER JUDGMENTS

First, what public records can you expect to find on your credit profile? A credit report is used to show three types of heinous public records. But not any longer. You may have heard or made wild guesses about this, but according to the source, only one type of public record is displayed in a credit report: bankruptcy. But, before we get there, you should be aware that, while bankruptcy is the only record displayed on your profile, it is not the only one to be concerned about.

Foreclosure is also critical. We'll start there, and then we'll look at how to handle the records on your profile. Let's get started:

WHAT EXACTLY IS FORECLOSURE?

The term "foreclosure" refers to an official situation in which a lender takes possession of an asset that was designated as collateral when applying for a loan. This means that foreclosure occurs when a debtor seizes property or assets to sell after the lender fails to repay the money borrowed.

Even though foreclosure has no effect on your credit score, you should avoid it at all costs. Whatever you used as collateral had to be something valuable to you. Probably your house (mortgage), your land parcels, or a vehicle you require for work or family responsibilities. It's heartbreaking to see those things go.

Foreclosure is also a lengthy and arduous process. It could last up to 700 days.

As a result, lenders try to avoid it whenever possible. Foreclosure typically occurs in a variety of formats. Some are referred to as Judicial, while others are referred to as Non-Judicial.

The primary distinction is that judicial foreclosure requires the lender to obtain official court approval before auctioning or seizing the property. The lender is not required to obtain court permissions in non-judicial cases. They only need to seize their assets.

The simplest way to avoid foreclosure, as with any other loan, is to pay your loans on time.

BANKRUPTCY NOW

Bankruptcy is a financial declaration that a person is no longer able to repay his debts. It is a court-proven declaration that a debtor has tried and failed to obtain the funds owed to them.

And now, all creditors must be patient with them. It appears to be a method of obtaining debt relief in some way, if not all.

Bankruptcy laws were enacted after a long period in which lenders could be stigmatized for life, forced into slavery, or passed down to their children.

When you declare bankruptcy these days, you are required to declare all of your assets. For example, if you declare bankruptcy with an outstanding balance of $80,000, you will list all of your personal belongings and assets from your homes, such as chairs, dresses, and artwork. It is then the creditor's responsibility to determine whether some of those items have value and can be sold, seized, or not. As it turns out, many people lose more than they expected when they declare bankruptcy, making it a win-win situation for creditors.

Of course, debtors realize this before it's too late. This is why many people try to tamper with the records and make false statements or declarations in order to conceal their assets. These actions are classified as Bankruptcy Fraud in the United States and are strictly prohibited. If you file for bankruptcy, be prepared to face all of the ramifications.

Bankruptcy is filed when a debtor declares that she is unable to repay any additional loans. She has exhausted all other options and is now forced to seek leniency from the court.

When this is approved, the debtor declares all of his or her assets, which are then liquidated, or sold, to pay off any outstanding loans.

Following that, the debtor is completely relieved of any further payments. The only problem is that it affects your credit score for ten years in a row.

This means that any potential creditor will understand that you were in a financial bind at some point and had to give things that did not correspond to the loan's value. That is never a good sign, and it may be the reason you are unable to obtain a loan in the following years.

Bankruptcy is declared when a debtor is confident that he can pay his debts but, due to his current financial situation, it will take a long time to do so. This period could last several years. Finally, the court approves a repayment plan, and the debtor pays over that time period. After making payments, he is debt-free. Bankruptcy appears on your credit report for a period of seven years. It receives a lot of criticism, and it could be one of the reasons you're turned down, but it's unlikely.

Only a company or individual who is unable to fully honor its financial obligations or make payments to its creditor's files for bankruptcy.

This means that filing for bankruptcy is a legal action taken by a company or individual to relieve themselves of debt obligations, in which all outstanding debt of the company is evaluated and paid from the company's assets. Bankruptcy is a legal procedure that is used to free individuals and businesses from debt that they have already incurred while also providing creditors with the opportunity to get their debts paid. It is said to provide a fresh start by forgiving unplayable debts while also providing creditors with a substantial opportunity to obtain repayment methods based on a person's or business's available assets that can be liquidated.

In theory, this means that the ability to file for bankruptcy can benefit an entire economy by providing businesses and individuals with a second chance to gain maximum access to consumer credit and by providing creditors with a reliable measure of debt repayment. Once the bankruptcy proceeding is completed successfully, the debtor will be released from their obligation to repay the debt incurred prior to filing for bankruptcy.

However, the fact that such a person has previously acquired debts and filed for bankruptcy will be reflected on their credit report. This information will be kept on file for seven to ten years, depending on the type of bankruptcy filed.

BANKRUPTCY TYPES

Bankruptcy can be classified into two types.

Debt Repayment

This is simply debt cancellation as a result of bankruptcy. According to the Internal Revenue Code, a debtor must include the discharge of indebtedness in their gross income, after which a court must have discharged his/her debt if all conditions are met.

However, if a debtor refuses financial counseling, commits a crime, fails to fully explain the loss of his/her assets, provides false information during court proceedings, or otherwise disobeys the court's orders, a judge has the right to refuse to discharge such a person's debt.

The Payment Strategy

This is a type of bankruptcy filed in which a debtor and his or her lawyer submit to the court a repayment plan outlining how the debtor intends to pay off his or her debts over the next three to five years. This plan is based on the debtor's income, food and utility expenses, taxes, and healthcare costs.

If the court approves the plan, the debtor begins making the payments specified in the plan. If such a debtor makes timely payments, the remaining debts will be discharged at the end of the three to five-year period. The payments are made to a trustee appointed by the bankruptcy court, who then pays the creditors while receiving a commission.

IN BUSINESS, THERE ARE TWO TYPES OF BANKRUPTCY:

Bankruptcy Reorganization

This is a type of bankruptcy that is filed to assist business owners who have serious problems with their business but still have regular income and valuable assets in reorganizing the business. The company is allowed to continue operations, under the supervision of the court, of course.

During the supervision, creditors are not permitted to interfere with the debtors. Business owners must share their reorganization plan with creditors and pay them a portion of the proceeds. However, if the creditors do not agree with the plan, they have the option of filing a competing plan.

Farming Insolvency

It is a type of bankruptcy designed specifically for farmers from the same family.

Its purpose is to assist the family in reorganizing their farming business and repaying all of their debts.

The unpredictability of farming and seasonal trends are serious considerations.

THE ESSENTIALS OF CREDIT CARD DEBT AND BANKRUPTCY

People understand the fundamentals of credit cards. After being approved, you will receive your card and activate it. It can be used for almost anything, such as purchasing groceries, clothing, or paying bills.

The good news is that you only need to make the minimum payment each month to stay out of credit card debt. Unfortunately, it is this type of thinking that frequently leads to credit card debt.

The following are some fundamental points about credit card debt that most people are unaware of.

Understand when short-term loans make more sense.

Sometimes we need cash fast or a way to pay a few bills quickly. For these reasons, many people use credit cards. They receive an approval within minutes, and their card will be mailed to them within five to seven business days. However, it is sometimes preferable to visit your bank and speak with a loan advisor. If you need a couple of thousand dollars to pay off your medical bills before they are sent to a collection agency, you should consider taking out a short-term loan from your local bank or credit union.

Credit card debt can harm your credit.

Paying off your credit cards late or missing the minimum payment aren't the only things that will result in you having bad credit; having credit cards with high balances can also increase your chances of having bad credit. This is why you should never max out your credit cards. You should keep at least 30% of your credit limit available at all times.

While it is nearly impossible in today's world, your best chance of avoiding bad credit is to stay out of debt as much as possible.

The easy part is owing; the difficult part is repaying credit cards.

The reality of life is that you never know what will happen.

You could work for a company for decades and then be laid off at random due to budget cuts. You could have an illness flare-up that necessitates surgery.

There are numerous circumstances that can cause you to miss credit card payments and be unable to pay your bills.

You may also find it difficult to pay the full minimum balance, so you may decide to pay only half of it each month.

You will discover that you are spending more than you are earning.

It makes no difference how responsible you are with credit cards; one of the main reasons people get into credit card debt is because they spend more than they earn each month.

Credit cards are very appealing because they give you the impression that you can simply pay them back later or make smaller payments on the purchase every month.

In reality, however, you should never spend more than your monthly income.

The majority of people use credit cards to deal with emergencies.

People frequently tell others that a credit card should only be used in an emergency, but do you know what a true emergency is? The majority of people live paycheck to paycheck. As a result, when their checking account balance falls below a certain threshold, and there are several days until their next payday, they will begin to reconsider each purchase they make and wonder if they should use their credit card because it is considered an emergency or a need. The best thing you can do is start slowly saving a portion of your paycheck and putting it into an emergency fund account.

People believe that as long as they pay the bare minimum, they will be fine.

In reality, you should always pay more than the minimum payment. Consider this: if you make a $75 minimum payment, at least 25% of your payment will go toward interest and fees. This means that you are only putting 75% of your payment toward debt repayment. This could be a small amount depending on how much you owe. If you are not careful, you may find yourself exceeding your credit limit, in which case your credit card company will charge you an over-limit fee.

Furthermore, paying only the minimum payment will take years to pay off. It makes no difference how low you believe your credit limit is compared to how high you believe your minimum monthly payment is. Even if you stop using your credit card, it could take at least a couple of years to pay off your debt.

BANKRUPTCY IMPLICATIONS

Before you consider filing for bankruptcy, you should first understand how it works, as well as the benefits and drawbacks. It is not a simple issue that can be resolved quickly, but rather one with a complex side that only a bankruptcy attorney understands. It is best if you gather as much information as possible before declaring bankruptcy. The following are the ramifications of declaring bankruptcy.

PROS

Debt discharge: One of the main reasons people file for bankruptcy is to get their debts discharged. And when such debt is discharged, it erases all of your debts and prevents creditors from collecting additional payments from you; the debtor feels relieved. It's a significant benefit of declaring bankruptcy.

Not everyone who applies for debt relief is successful. Filing for bankruptcy if you owe money for alimony, taxes, or child support is a waste of time. These debts are neither forgiven nor discharged.

Automatic Stay: This is yet another benefit of filing for bankruptcy. It is a situation in which the person who files for bankruptcy is automatically protected from creditors as well as the collection of debts. The injunction remains in effect until the court orders that the debts be honored, forgiven, or discharged. In the case of divorce proceedings, the automatic stay may be lifted.

CONS

Property Loss: A bankruptcy filer's property may be forfeited if the court determines it is valuable enough to pay off the debt.

This will occur if you include your property in your bankruptcy case to the bankruptcy trustee. Your creditor would have more clout in attempting to seize your property, especially if you used it as collateral initially.

Credit Score: Another disadvantage of declaring bankruptcy is that it lowers your credit score. When loaners check your credit history, they will only see you as risky because filing for bankruptcy will not clean up your debt history, even if your debt is canceled. However, it is preferable to incurring debt. You can always work on improving your credit score later.

Privacy: If you value your privacy, filing for bankruptcy may not be for you, which is why you must conduct thorough research if you intend to file for bankruptcy.

You can either prepare for the consequences or seek alternative solutions. When you file for bankruptcy, every detail of your financial statements is made public. In other words, anyone with access to your personal information can do so without your knowledge. Anyone can easily assess the amount you owed, who your creditors were, and your bankruptcy schedule. If you value your privacy, this can be a very good deal.

SO, WHAT CAN YOU DO TO KEEP IT?

Prevention has always been preferable to cure. But if you're already here, dwelling on your blunder isn't going to help. Get back on your feet and prepare to make a better impression in future endeavors.

Try to pay off your other debts as soon as possible. The better you perform in other debts, the more likely you are to mitigate the effects of bankruptcy on your profile.

Passivity in Building Rather Than Activities

This is not explicitly stated anywhere, but it is common sense. Increasing assets improves dependability. You will be able to mortgage your resources for credit if you have enough of them. As a result, creditors will give you credit in exchange for a good guarantee in exchange for their risk.

Avoid construction liabilities such as credit card bills, as they will have a negative impact on your rating.

Maintain contact with financial institutions.

Always be honest about your financial situation and maintain good relations with your creditors. Always stay in touch with them and express your inability to pay, if applicable, and see if an agreement can be reached in any way.

After all, they want their money, not a drop in their rating.

IMPROVING CREDIT STANDARDS AFTER FORECLOSURE

Foreclosure can significantly lower a consumer's credit score. If you have had the unfortunate experience of going through a foreclosure, the following article will explain how to rebuild your credit score.

A drop in house price, followed by a recession, and a high unemployment rate have caused a number of people to fall behind on their mortgage payments. As a result of failing to pay capital and interest on home loans, bankruptcies and foreclosures ensued. Because consumer payment history is one of the most important factors influencing credit score calculation, a foreclosure obviously had a negative impact on the credit rating of all those who lost their homes. As a result, the topic of improving credit scores after a foreclosure has gained prominence.

If the mortgage deed contains a sales clause, a creditor can initiate the foreclosure procedure and complete the entire process outside of the court system. In the absence of a sales clause power, the lender is forced to sue the borrower. In other words, judicial foreclosure is a foregone conclusion. Regardless of the nature of the proceedings, the details are public records and appear on the consumer's credit report. For a period of seven years, the information remains firmly embedded in the consumer's credit report. As previously stated, following a foreclosure sale, the consumer's credit score drops from 350 to 400 points.

Although having a blemished credit report and a low credit score is a double whammy, many creditors recognize the consumer's efforts to improve credit scores. Good credit scores are required to obtain loans at a low-interest rate, to obtain insurance, and to apply for jobs that require the applicant to assume managerial and financial responsibilities.

Enhance your post-foreclosure credit score

To improve your credit score after a foreclosure, you should apply for installment or revolving credit and make it a habit to pay interest on a regular basis. Establishing a track record of on-time payments can go a long way toward improving a consumer's credit score. A consumer who wants to improve their credit scores after bankruptcy can take the same approach.

Credit cards that are guaranteed

People can use secured credit cards to rebuild their credit because they can be approved for them within six months of a foreclosure sale or discharge failure. These credit cards are backed by a CD that serves as a guarantee for credit card companies. Typically, the credit line is 50 to 100 percent of the deposit amount. Repaying the entire credit card balance on a monthly basis will result in the credit card company extending additional credit lines to the consumer without further deposits as collateral. If the consumer makes timely payments, a secured credit card will be converted to an unsecured credit card within 18 months.

FHA-insured loans

People who have had their homes foreclosed on must wait three years from the date of the foreclosure sale to apply for an FHA-insured loan. Assuming the consumer is approved for a secured credit card and raises his or her credit score to 620 points, FHA secured loans can serve as a springboard for further credit score improvement. The Federal Housing Administration (FHA) provides secured government mortgages, which protect the lender if the homeowner defaults on the mortgage. As a result, the consumer can benefit from a down mortgage by paying only 3.5 percent of the home's purchase price.

These measures are not only beneficial to consumers who want to improve their credit scores after a foreclosure, but they are also necessary for people who want to improve their credit rating after a debt settlement because a debt settlement does not completely cancel out information from the consumer credit report. The end result is a favorable credit report and credit scores.

When you apply for one of these services with bad credit, you are required to pay a deposit. Because you need deposits for all of your bills, moving into a new place becomes more expensive. Repairing your credit will result in a higher credit score, which will allow you to avoid these deposits.

CHAPTER 12

How Do I Raise My Credit Limit?

CHECK YOUR CREDIT REPORTS TO MAKE SURE THEY ARE ACCURATE AND FREE OF ERRORS! Each of us has three credit reports.

Trans Union, Equifax, and Experian are among them. Credit reports are not always accurate, and many of them contain mistakes.

One-fifth of the population has an error on at least one of their credit reports. You can check your credit score in a variety of ways. According to the Fair Credit Reporting Act, you are entitled to one free credit report from each of the three major credit reporting agencies each year. Below is a list of websites where you can check your credit for free:

- http://www.creditkarma.com/
- http://www.freecreditreport.com/
- http://www.experian.com/
- http://www.annualcreditreport.com/

Some credit card companies even provide a free credit report. I have a Capital One credit card that allows me to check my credit for free because I have an account with them. When it comes to credit accuracy, there are numerous factors to consider. Here is a list of questions to help you identify potential errors.

Is all of my personal information correct?

Is it true that all of my credit accounts have been reported?

Are there any references to missed or late payments that you actually paid on time?

Are there any accounts or applications that you are unfamiliar with?

Simply ensure that the information on your report is correct.

A clean credit report is essential for a high credit score.

SET UP YOUR BALANCES

The amount of money you owe makes up 30% of your credit report.

Paying down your balances will definitely improve your credit score, but it won't happen overnight. The keyword here is patience. Most people believe that paying off a balance immediately raises your credit score. That is simply not true. It usually takes 30 days or more to notice an improvement.

SET UP NEW ACCOUNTS

Now, applying for a slew of different credit cards is not the plan here. Check to see if you are eligible to open a new account. Credit Karma comes in handy for this. CK suggests new credit cards you can apply for based on your current credit score, as well as the likelihood of approval for each. This reduces your chances of being denied and further damaging your credit, as applying for credit and being denied is a black mark on your credit.

Don't be discouraged if you are rejected. This will only have a minor impact on your credit score. That is why it is critical to be aware of your credit score in order to determine whether you have a good chance of being approved for a new credit card or loan. Having more accounts diversifies your credit report. That's great! The more types of credit you demonstrate responsibility for, the higher your credit score will be. However, you must exercise extreme caution! Make certain that you keep up with all of your payments.

EXTEND YOUR CREDIT LIMIT

If you have bad credit, you usually get whatever you deposit for your credit limit. For example, if someone applies for and is approved for a secured credit card, a deposit is usually required. Their initial credit limit will be determined by the amount they pay as a deposit, such as $300. Of course, after a while, you'll want to buy more expensive items. You don't want a low limit because it will be much easier to max out the card. This is a major issue for credit. After you have been responsible and made all of your payments on time with your current credit card, apply for a credit increase. Here are some suggestions for increasing your credit limit.

Choose an existing card that you already own for the limit increase.

Do not be greedy; instead, request a reasonable increase to demonstrate that you are responsible and understand credit.

Make your case, but don't appear desperate. Apply with confidence if you have been making on-time payments, using the correct amount of credit, your income has increased, or you have always paid the minimum balance.

Wait for the appropriate moment to ask. I would recommend waiting 4–6 months before requesting a limit increase. During those months, you must ensure that you are making responsible use of your loans. Accounts are typically reviewed every six months by credit issuers. In fact, people in good standing are more likely to get a higher limit increase without even asking.

OBTAIN A SECURED CREDIT CARD OR LOAN

As previously stated, secured credit cards are ideal for people attempting to build or rebuild their credit. A secured credit card functions similarly to a regular credit card. The difference with secured credit cards is that they require a cash collateral deposit, which becomes the account's line of credit. If you've had trouble getting approved for an unsecured credit card in the past, a secured card might be a good option for you. Secured loans work in the same way. These loans are available from a variety of banks and credit unions. They are an excellent way to improve your credit.

DO NOT APPLY FOR TOO MANY POSITIONS AT THE SAME TIME.

If you decide to apply for a credit card, give it some time before applying for another. Problems can arise if you attempt to use a large amount of credit at once. This can make you appear desperate and in desperate need of money.

Many stores provide in-store credit and will give you a discount if you sign up for it. If you are not prepared, this can hurt your score!

These store credits will result in a "hard inquiry" on your credit report, which may have a negative impact if you are not approved. If you are denied, work on improving your score before applying again. 3–6 months is a good amount of time to space out credit applications.

GET RID OF YOUR COLLECTIONS AND DEROGATORY MARKS.

Contact debt collectors to see if they are willing to stop reporting to credit bureaus in exchange for a payment plan. Debt collectors will usually settle for less than the full amount if you speak with them and reach an agreement. It may be difficult to recover if you have a lot of damage.

Paying down your debts, on the other hand, will boost your credit score. Furthermore, once balances are paid in full, most credit card companies will remove negative marks from your report. This increases your chances of obtaining new credit and improving your credit score.

REDUCE YOUR CREDIT UTILIZATION RATE

Assume you have a credit card with a $10,000 limit. If you spent $5,000 on something, you would have a credit utilization of 50%. However, if you spend the entire $10,000 on something, you will have a credit utilization of 100 percent. Have you gotten the picture? Many people simply do not understand the significance of maintaining the proper ratio. The important figure to remember is 30%! This is the ideal number to keep in mind when it comes to credit limits. Spend no more than $3,000 if your budget is $10,000. Spend no more than $60 if your budget is $200. Simply multiply your credit limit by 0.3 to get your figure. To maintain a good credit score, try to keep your debts below 30% of your total income.

These eight tips will arm you with the knowledge you need to reclaim your life. Make these decisions as soon as possible. Your credit is crucial, and these eight tips will help you improve it before you know it!

CHAPITRE 13

Should You Hire a Credit Repair Company?

Getting the right financial education and knowing what is best for you is the best way to manage your credit responsibly. This will take some time and effort on your part to learn how everything works. However, because your credit scores are so important in managing your accounts and saving money, you should learn everything you can about the credit bureaus that create credit appraisals. To help you get started, here are some key facts about TransUnion, Experian, and Equifax, the three major credit bureaus in the United States:

TRANSUNION

TransUnion has offices all over the country that handle various aspects of credit, such as identity theft, credit management, and other credit issues, as well as different types of credit customers, such as personal, business, and press inquiries. If you find errors on your TransUnion credit report, you can dispute them by calling 800.916.8800 or visiting their website. If you believe you are a victim of identity theft, contact them at 800.680.7289 as soon as possible.

EXPERIAN

Experian, like other credit bureaus, offers a wide range of administrations for individuals, businesses, and the media. Experian is headquartered in Costa Mesa, California, and operates a website. If you find errors in your report or need to report potential identity theft, this credit bureau makes it more difficult to contact them via phone. Instead, they encourage visitors to use online forms for questions, identity theft reports, and other concerns.

EQUIFAX

Equifax, headquartered in Atlanta, GA, has several departments to assist customers with a wide range of questions and concerns. Their website is also set up to allow people to use online forms to work on errors, report identity theft, and handle other issues. In any case, if a person believes their identity has been stolen, they can call Equifax at 888.397.3742 to report it. If you find an error, you can also call their phone number and speak with someone who can fix it for you.

These are the three credit bureaus in the country, and they each use different methods to allow people to contact them with questions or to resolve any issues they may be having. Rather than contacting the credit bureaus directly, some people prefer to use a credit checking administration to help them manage their credit and stay on top of their finances. Although the credit bureaus all have related projects, most people prefer to work with an independent organization to help them with these issues. As a result, they receive an unbiased assessment of their credit score as well as a plethora of additional services to help them manage and improve their credit ratings on a proactive basis.

GETTING THE MOST OUT OF CREDIT BUREAUS

It is critical to understand that all three credit bureaus have sensitive financial information. However, there is no way to prevent lenders and collection agencies from sharing your information with the companies listed above. You can limit any potential problems with credit bureaus by reviewing your credit reports annually and acting quickly if you notice any errors. It's also a good idea to keep an eye on your credit cards and other open credit products to make sure no one is abusing the accounts. If you have a card that you do not frequently use, sign up for alerts on that card so that you are notified if any transactions occur, and review statements for your active tickets on a regular basis.

Following that, if you notice any signs of fraud or theft, you can place a credit freeze with the three credit bureaus and be diligent in tracking the activity of your credit card in the future.

HOW DO THE BUREAUS OBTAIN THEIR INFORMATION?

To understand how the score is calculated, we must first understand all of the different inputs to your score, i.e., where the bureaus get their information. You may have several factors that report information to credit bureaus or none at all. Credit bureaus refer to credit cards as revolving accounts or revolving debt. Payments and balances are reported each month, as well as any late payments. This means that any cards bearing your name will be reported to all bureaus. This includes cards from a spouse or parent. If you are an authorized user on the account, it will always be reported on your credit. Many people's credit has been ruined as a result of a spouse or parent declaring bankruptcy or failing to pay their credit card bills. If your name appears on any credit card belonging to people who may not pay their bills, request that your name be removed immediately!

Installment loans also report data to credit bureaus. An installment loan would be if you went to your local Sears and financed a washer/dryer set with a down payment.

The total balance of these loans, as well as the timeliness and amounts of your monthly payments, are all reported. If you have a mortgage or student loan, that information is disclosed. The total amount owed, the total amount paid thus far, and the status of monthly payments are all reported. This data is tracked and organized in their databases.

Conclusion

Thank you once more for purchasing this book! I hope this book was able to assist you with your needs and answer your questions about credit scores.

You now have the knowledge to help you build better credit and raise your credit score. Some of these strategies may not be appropriate for your situation or if you have already tried them. Hopefully, you discovered a few new strategies to try and will be able to achieve the credit score status you desire.

It will take time for those who have experienced a financial setback, such as years of arrears or bankruptcy. Regardless of whether someone provides you with good credit lines until then, it takes ten years for the bankruptcy to leave your credit history and no longer affect you. If you had a bankruptcy, it could take up to ten years to get back into the 800s, and some people will not make it because they do not use the credit-building options outlined in this book.

Anyone who has not maintained a long history with various types of credit may also have difficulty obtaining a score above 800. However, there are fewer steps you can take to improve your credit scores.

Simply paying attention to the credit types you have, ensuring that you open new accounts, keep old accounts open, and establish a long history with consistent and reliable payments, as well as a small "amount owed" in comparison to your income and credit limits, is all that is required.

If you are willing to put in the effort, you can have a decent, if not better, credit score. If necessary, use family to begin acquiring new credit lines. Make certain that if you are using credit to build your score, you are going home and paying that purchase off right away by depositing the funds in your account. Only a steady, reliable, and consistent credit history will provide a "great credit" appearance, as well as higher scores.

Because you now have the tools, there is no better time than now to get started on building great credit and increasing those scores.

As I've demonstrated throughout this book, even a moderately successful credit repair can provide you with a plethora of advantages. All that matters is that you put in the effort to try. If you go through this process and resolve some issues, you will only need to do it again in a few years. You already know what to look for and have some experience in approaching creditors and credit reporting agencies.

The benefits of credit repair may take some time to become apparent, but by carefully following all of the steps outlined in this book, you will eventually clear your credit and increase your chances of receiving higher scores on a credit application. It will also assist you in finding work, even if your credit is not completely repaired. When someone is evaluating your credit report and sees the written statements and all of the work you have put in, it shows how responsible and diligent you are about your finances and reveals a lot about who you are.

I hope that this book has not only persuaded you of the benefits of credit repair but also that it has provided a simple and clear explanation of the steps you must take in order to do so successfully. I wanted to make credit repair accessible to everyone and to recommend the best approach for a variety of problems. Many people are enthusiastic about credit repair, but when they see the effort and time required on the road to good credit, they become discouraged and give up. Others give up after receiving the first negative response from a creditor or credit reporting agency, and some even go through with it but stop doing things to improve their credit once they've completed the process and haven't been able to fix all of the negative items.

Damage control is just as important as the process itself, and as I mentioned in the section of the book dedicated to it, it has numerous long-term benefits. The most important aspect of the entire process is to stay motivated and to keep improving.

So, what are your plans for the future? The next step is to start putting what you've learned in this eBook to use in your current situation and working as hard as you can to start repairing your credit. What do you have to lose? If you simply take one step forward every day, you will be closer to your goal than you were before. It's the same as anything else in life: you get what you put in—wishing you the best of luck!

Established business credit adds value to the company. Any potential future sale of the business will benefit greatly if the business already has a positive business credit profile.

The higher the profile and the greater the depth of trade lines, the more valuable the business becomes to investors and other parties who may be interested in purchasing it in the future.

A good business credit profile and score can be built much more quickly than a business owner's personal credit profile.

Furthermore, business credit approvals typically have higher dollar amounts than personal credit approvals.

Business credit accounts typically have higher credit limits. It is simpler and faster to obtain approval from multiple credible sources.

Individual business credit approvals make it easier to get approved for multiple credit cards or credit lines than consumer credit approvals.

These are just a few of the numerous advantages that establishing business credit offers a company and its owner. For all of these reasons, it is difficult for any business to be truly successful unless it establishes a good business credit profile and score and uses it to help the business prosper.

You now have the knowledge and tools you need to ensure that your company can obtain and maintain an excellent business credit profile and score. Use your knowledge today to begin building business credit for your company or using business credit to help you start a new business venture.

You can finally have the positive business credit and financial future you deserve once you've established a positive business credit profile.

www.ingramcontent.com/pod-product-compliance
Lightning Source LLC
Chambersburg PA
CBHW071347230926
51846CB00002B/475